A BOOK OF HORS D'OEUVRE

A BOOK OF
HORS D'OEUVRE

Lucy G. Allen

ILLUSTRATED

BRAMHALL HOUSE · NEW YORK

*This edition published by Bramhall House,
a division of Clarkson N. Potter, Inc., by
arrangement with Little, Brown & Company.*
(A)

CONTENTS

I   A Chat about Hors d'Oeuvre   3

II   Hors d'Oeuvre Foods and Garnishes; to
       Make Canapés   7

     A List of Foods Used for Hors d'Oeuvre   7

     Types of Hors d'Oeuvre   13

     To Make Canapés   15

     Garnishes for Hors d'Oeuvre   18

     Accompaniments for Hors d'Oeuvre   20

III   Flavored Butters   21

IV   Canapés for Cocktails   27

     Fish   28

     Meat   41

     Cheese   50

     Miscellaneous   56

V   Pierced Savories   59

     Fish   60

     Meat   64

     Cheese   68

     Miscellaneous   71

VI   Hors d'Oeuvre for the Compartment Dish   75

     Dry Savories   75

     Moist Savories   80

Contents

VII	Spreads for Self-Service	89
VIII	First-Course or Table Hors d'Oeuvre	97
IX	Miscellaneous Recipes	108
	Dressings	116
X	Varied Combinations for Serving Hors d'Oeuvre	120
	Centerpieces for Platters of Hors d'Oeuvre	120
	Centerpieces for Pierced Savories	122
	Platter Arrangements of Hors d'Oeuvre	125
	Tray Combinations for Assorted Canapés	128
	Index	133

ILLUSTRATIONS

Pierced Savories Inserted in Grapefruit   *Frontispiece*

Utensils and Molds for Making Hors d'Oeuvre   16

Compartment Tray of Assorted Hors d'Oeuvre   17

Tray Service of Cocktail Canapés   46

Individual Cocktail Tray for Bridge Service   47

A Close-Up of Canapés   56

Assorted Hors d'Oeuvre   57

Hors d'Oeuvre Platter   78

A BOOK OF HORS D'OEUVRE

I

A CHAT ABOUT HORS D'OEUVRE

AN hors d'oeuvre or appetizer is a small portion of highly seasoned and flavored food formerly used to precede a meal and now used for many occasions. The custom of serving these relishes is a foreign one appreciated and adopted by Americans who have spent much time abroad and even by those who haven't. Each country has a distinctive type of hors d'oeuvre.

Italy sends us assorted relishes preserved in oil and called "antipasto" which are removed from the container, drained, and often, though not always, arranged upon a bed of lettuce. The Italians pour a French dressing over these relishes and sometimes rub the dish upon which they are served with a clove of garlic. If the dish should appear rather colorless from the selection chosen, it may be garnished with fancifully cut radishes or strips of pimiento to give a bright effect.

In Norway and Sweden we find the hors d'oeuvre set up on a table called "The *Smörgåsbord*" and making really a quite substantial meal, with smoked and pickled fish predominating and also highly seasoned meat dishes, some jellied and some hot, such as meat balls in a sauce.

The Germans use various kinds of sausage and rather heavy salads like potato or shredded vegetable, frequently combining herring with them.

Russia suggests caviar, the salted and sometimes the fresh (which is mildly salted) roe of the sturgeon; but other relishes are used, principally smoked and pickled fish.

France sends us sardines, *pâté de foie gras,* pickled vegetables and also different kinds of sausage.

In England one finds savories served at the close of the meal. These are usually hot and rich like small cheese soufflés or deviled fish dishes of crab, shrimp, etc.

Hors d'oeuvre have grown tremendously in popularity and are now used to accompany cocktails, to add zest to a buffet spread or as an outstanding feature of snack parties — in fact the less heavy ones frequently take the place of sandwiches at afternoon teas. Another use for assorted hors d'oeuvre is at the Sunday-night supper where they can be quite the important item on the menu, followed by one hot dish such as cheese soufflé, Italian spaghetti or scalloped fish. With fruit for a finish this makes an interesting meal, or for a simpler service two or three kinds of hors d'oeuvre accompanied by dark bread sandwiches and coffee may be brought to the living room.

Never hesitate to assemble a platter of odds and ends, for if attractively arranged they will have the appeal of assorted hors d'oeuvre — a few slices of ham, two rows of sliced dressed tomatoes, pats of cottage cheese, mounds of salad, cole slaw or cold cooked vegetables, highly seasoned with great care, for if they are not piquant the purpose is lost. The very first requisite for making successful appetizers is imagination, plus whatever happens to be on the shelves of the refrigerator or the pantry.

For snack parties have platters or chop plates set up with some attractive center arrangement and around that place hors d'oeuvre, selecting of course what can be easily eaten from the fingers, or one may serve relishes from compartment dishes. Popular for the snack party are bowls of spreads with wafers near at hand, also plates of neatly shaped bread to be toasted; or very much liked are the plates of wafer-thin sliced bread with crusts removed. One spreads these with some relish, folding them over once after spreading. A coffee percolator ready to be attached to the electric current should be provided, as well as whatever cold drinks one wishes to serve.

For the small occasion it is best to buy some of the excellently prepared assortments which come in bottles and jars as they furnish variety with little expense. Hors d'oeuvre packages may be purchased in all the smart food shops, but one can readily make appetizing spreads with eggs, ham, cheese and the simple foods. It depends upon how they are seasoned and combined whether they are satisfactory or not. It is a very good plan to mix some of the prepared pastes with cream cheese as this modifies sharpness or intensity of flavor and also extends the mixture. On any occasion avoid serving too many varieties as the average family would not find it feasible to offer the assortment one sees at a hotel or a club. Even though trays of decorated canapés are pleasing to look at it is best not to make fussy ones in great number, if at all, especially if you are putting the party together by yourself. As most canapés and hors d'oeuvre are best made at the eleventh hour and since that hour is apt to be the busiest one of the day, the popular hors d'oeuvre are those which can be prepared in the briefest period of time.

II

HORS D'OEUVRE FOODS AND GARNISHES; TO MAKE CANAPÉS

A LIST OF FOODS USED FOR HORS D'OEUVRE

Anchovy Fillets (rolled and flat)
Anchovy Paste
Antipasto
Artichoke Bottoms (large in cans; small in oil)
Aspic Jelly
Avocado
Bacon
Cabbage (finely shaved)
Capers
Caviar
Celery
Cheese (many varieties)
Chicken
Chutney
Crab Meat
Cress
Eggs (hard-boiled)
Finnan Haddie
Ham
Herring Fillets
Horse-radish Root (fresh)
Lemons
Liver (both chicken and calves')
Lobster
Meats (deviled or potted)
Mushrooms
Olives (ripe, green and stuffed)
Oysters
Parsley
Pâté de Foie Gras
Peppers (green and red)
Pickled English Walnuts
Pickled Watermelon Rind
Pickles (many varieties, including Mustard)
Pimientos

Prunes   Shrimp
Radishes   Smoked Salmon
Rose Apples   Smoked Turkey Paste
Sardines   Tomatoes
Sausages (many varieties)   Tuna Fish

Many pastes come in jars ready for spreading and they are especially good for the emergency shelf or in case you do not care to prepare them yourself.

Anchovies

Anchovies are tiny silvery fishes caught in the Mediterranean. The most famous come from Gorgona, a small island near Leghorn, where they are caught in nets as they come in from the deeper waters for the purpose of spawning. They are preserved whole as well as in the form of paste and essence. The pastes are prepared by pressing the fish through a sieve and adding simple flavoring and some oil. The essences consist of the fish steeped in highly spiced brine or pickle, then strained and bottled.

Antipasto

Antipasto is a choice relish to be served with little trouble and is a help when there are unexpected guests. The jars and tins vary as to contents but usually have tuna fish, artichoke bottoms, pickles, olives, peppers, goose liver and some vegetables.

Capers

Capers are the unopened flowers of a low trailing shrub. It grows wild in some places but in France is cultivated. Only the small, grayish-green flower buds have commercial value. They have an aromatic and pungent flavor and are usually preserved in tarragon vinegar. The smallest buds are considered the choicest.

Caviar

Caviar should be kept on ice for three hours before serving. It should be seasoned with lemon juice and cayenne or else passed with quarters of lemon and cayenne. As metal affects the flavor of caviar it is best to use a wooden fork or spoon for mixing. It may be served on toast, from a block of ice, in a stuffed egg or on a slice of egg, and also from a dish. In the latter case, a small dish containing minced, hard-boiled egg and one of finely chopped onion are also passed. Be sure that the caviar is very cold and the toast to accompany it very hot and dry.

Chutney

Chutney is a pickle originally made in India, which is still the source of the finest grades. It is sweet and hot, having for its content mangoes, ginger, raisins, chilis, spices and other ingredients.

Consommé

Consommé in small tins is a convenient meat stock to use for aspic jelly, especially Consommé Madrilène; then too one may purchase a canned aspic ready for use. Tomato aspic is given in many of the following recipes because it is so satisfactory. It is light amber in color, sparkling, and the tomato gives an acid that is pleasing. The recipe will be found on page 115. To make red tomato jelly, follow the same rule, straining but not clearing the mixture.

Preserved Fish

Preserved fish should be wiped carefully, to remove the oil in which it is preserved, and then dressed with the best salad oil. If the fish is large, it should be cut into small portions.

Horse-radish Root

Fresh horse-radish root is far superior to anything that comes bottled. It can be bought in any of the large city markets at all seasons of the year and can be kept for weeks if properly cared for. Pare from the top end as much as will be needed, and grate. Wrap remaining, unprepared root in a wet cheesecloth and keep in the crisper of the refrigerator. The roots vary in size and are sold by the pound.

Olives

Olives come both green and ripe, and stuffed. Some are stuffed with anchovies, some with celery, some with almonds, but the most popular are those stuffed with sweet red pimiento.

Pâté de Foie Gras

Pâté de foie gras is made from the livers of geese especially fattened for the purpose. It can be bought in tin or in crockery pots. Remove the fat which is put over the top to preserve it and with a spoon which has been dipped into hot water cut the paste in thin slices. It can be served in many ways, but usually it is accompanied by aspic, which cuts the richness. It can be served in a simple way by placing the thin slices on a lettuce leaf and garnishing with meat jelly and parsley. The can should be chilled before opening and the *foie gras* chilled before serving.

Purée de Foie Gras

Purée de foie gras is canned like potted meat — the livers having been pressed through a fine sieve, well seasoned, and truffles added. It is especially good for spreading canapés.

Pickled English Walnuts

The green nuts are gathered before the enclosing nut shells harden and are pickled. They are black like a truffle, very sour, hot in taste, and make an effective garnish as well as a desirable relish.

Pimientos

The pimiento is a thick-meated Spanish pepper of good size which comes canned and is used much for flavor as well as color.

Rose Apples

Rose apples are sweet peppers the shape of a small, smooth tomato, very bright in color, firm and crisp. They are preserved in sugar and vinegar and can be bought in either tin or glass. They make dainty cases for most relishes.

Sausage and Ham

Sausage and ham should be thinly and evenly sliced.

Shrimp

A good canned shrimp is much better than a poor fresh one. Those which come in liquid, commercially called "wet shrimp," seem to give the best satisfaction.

Fresh shrimp should be boiled in water to which are added a slice of onion, a slice of lemon, a bit of bay leaf and salt — the time, from fifteen to twenty minutes.

Smoked Salmon

The smoked salmon which comes in tins labeled Lax is sliced much thinner than one could possibly slice it oneself. The native smoked salmon can be used satisfactorily but it cannot be kept on the emergency shelf as Lax can.

Tuna Fish

Tuna fish is caught in the Mediterranean and off our Pacific Coast and comes preserved in oil, and also canned. Cut it in thin slices and arrange neatly on the serving dish. Use a garnish of chopped parsley and capers, and dress with a little oil.

TYPES OF HORS D'OEUVRE

There are different types of hors d'oeuvre and when classified the right kind may be easily selected for the special occasion. The cocktail canapé is perhaps the most popular of all the appetizers. It consists of some savory mixture or relish spread or placed upon a firm, edible base, preferably toasted or fried bread, although occasionally pastry and wafers are used.

The skewered tidbits which we like to call "pierced savories" are much in favor and are usually inserted into some centerpiece although many persons prefer them placed upon the dish. They may also be arranged in bonbon cups with the picks uppermost. The savories are eaten from the pick, which is then discarded, so be sure that a suitable container is at hand to receive the skewers. Pretzel sticks and also potato sticks may sometimes be used in place of the picks and though not as dainty have the advantage of being edible.

Then we have piquant morsels to set up in a compartment dish and they may be of two kinds — dry and easy to eat from the fingers or moist savories to be served when plates and forks are used. Compartment dishes are shown in the specialty shops and they make attractive containers when the relishes are artistically combined.

For buffet spreads and especially for snack parties, bowls of various savory spreads are in order with toast, crackers, potato chips or whatever you fancy near by. Butter spreaders and plates will be found useful for this service. Also for the snack party, bowls of different dressings are placed on the table for dunking some of the pierced savories, such as shrimp, cubes of lobster, sprigs of cauliflower, etc. The dressings may be chosen from Russian, horse-radish, mayonnaise, a cooked mustard dressing and a French dressing made with outstanding seasonings such as curry or chutney.

For the spread where plates and forks are available one may use any type of hors d'oeuvre, especially the heartier relishes like stuffed eggs, stuffed tomatoes, etc.

A *smörgåsbord* supper calls for a great assortment of the heartiest appetizers as well as suitable accompaniments, such as brown-bread sandwiches, cress sandwiches, any canapés, Ry-Krisp, Melba toast, etc.

And finally there are hors d'oeuvre which are served as a first course at the table. These include some canapés which are not suitable for eating from the fingers, such as caviar on artichoke bottoms, and also small aspic molds, oysters in various ways or a savory like antipasto.

Relishes that are not arranged upon bread, such as

small stuffed tomatoes, tiny stuffed beets and small savory aspics, are served from platters, compartment dishes or upon individual plates. These will be found useful at buffet spreads, snack parties, or as a first course if cocktails are not served, and wafers or Melba toast should be an accompaniment.

When the compartment dish is used for first-course relishes, its contents should be moist and savory for table service, but for cocktail service they should be dryer and suitable for eating from the hand.

Occasionally one might like to serve assorted hors d'oeuvre individually — just three or four relishes arranged attractively upon each plate and served as a first course at luncheon.

TO MAKE CANAPÉS

Make small cuts from rather thin slices of bread — they may be plain squares, oblongs or triangles; or, using cutters, form round, oval, crescent, diamond or palm-leaf shapes. The cutters may have either plain or coarsely fluted edge.

There are different methods of crisping these foundations. They may be toasted (and some recipes call for only one side toasted); they may be buttered and placed on a cookie sheet to become brown and crisp in the oven, or they may be sautéed in either olive oil or butter. When you have many to prepare cover the bottom of a frying basket with the shapes and plunge into hot fat, draining them immediately on clean paper to absorb any excess fat. The bread crusts retain their crispness longer when using this method and it is used by those sending out canapés on order. When preparing only a few canapés, put olive oil into a small pan to the depth of one-half inch, spear bread on a fork and hold in the hot oil for a second, until brown and crisp.

The next step is to spread the canapés with a savory butter or a highly seasoned paste, sometimes both. On this butter or paste arrange bits of fish, meat or any appetizing food, or a garnish, taking care that neither flavors nor colors clash and also that decorations are simple and effective. It is a great mistake to combine many different flavors, and great stress should be laid upon the size of canapés and tasty bites, for if larger than a mouthful they are difficult to eat. It is also important that they should be well seasoned and neatly made.

The following browned bread cases furnish a crisp background easy to eat and are a change from a flat surface. Use a sheet of tiny cake tins, each section measuring one and one-half inches across. Slice white bread as thin as possible and cut into two-inch squares, brush over lightly with melted butter and fit them into the cake tins, pressing them in firmly; the points will extend slightly above the tin. Bake in a 400° F. oven until brown and crisp and fill with any preferred filling either cold or hot. They are only a mouthful and are

UTENSILS AND MOLDS FOR MAKING
HORS D'OEUVRE

COMPARTMENT TRAY OF ASSORTED
HORS D'OEUVRE

Cheese Truffles and Ripe Olives (*center*) — Pimiento Star Canapés —
Cheese and Olive Canapés II — Shrimp and Cress Canapés

most attractive. They can be made in advance and kept in the warming oven.

Very tiny forms of pâte à choux (choux paste) make interesting cases for fillings but they should be no larger than a fifty-cent piece if round, and very small if made into an elongated shape.

Melba toast and potato chips are also foundations for appetizers. To crisp the chips spread them out in a pan of considerable surface and place in a 350°F. oven before using. Spread only at the last moment as they soften quickly. It is really more satisfactory to have a large bowl of these chips near bowls of "spreads" and let guests help themselves than to serve them prepared beforehand.

A great many of the cold appetizers are improved in appearance by an application of aspic which gives a thin gelatin coating. This treatment is especially desirable when preparing hors d'oeuvre some time in advance as it keeps them from drying as well as giving an attractive gloss. Place the appetizers on a rack (a cake cooler is useful) and set it over a pan to catch what does not adhere to the shapes. Pour over these shapes, using a spoon, a partially chilled aspic to form a coating and then place in the refrigerator to set. Another method is to apply the aspic lightly with a pastry brush. One may use an aspic of cleared tomato juice, veal or chicken stock, or even a canned aspic. A canned Madrilène consommé makes a fine aspic, using one tablespoon of gelatin to one cup of liquid.

When serving hot hors d'oeuvre be sure they *are* hot and have them brought in on trays at frequent intervals.

GARNISHES FOR HORS D'OEUVRE

Almonds, salted (halves or minced)

Anchovies, rolled or fillets

Beets, pickled (require care in use as color spreads)

Butter, flavored (piped through bag and tube)

Capers

Carrots, grated

Caviar, placed as a tiny bunch of grapes, with parsley leaf and stem

Egg Yolk, sifted

English Pickled Walnuts, cut in sections or minced. They give an effective touch of black and also season well. Can replace truffle and are less expensive.

Lemon Slices or Shapes. Use with fish as a tart garnish. Cut a Maltese Cross and dust with paprika and minced parsley. Or, a slice from a notched lemon in center of which arrange two petals cut from a radish and two cut from a green pepper. Or, a half slice from a notched lemon and three small diamonds cut from a cooked beet on lemon.

Lobster-Claw Meat. Using the small side claw, slice across, making small thin ovals, white with a fine rim of red.

Lobster Coral

Olives, Ripe and Green, minced or cut in petal shape

Olives, Stuffed, cut in rings or halves

Onions, Pearl. Sometimes called Dutch Onions. They
come in different sizes.

Paprika. For an oblong canapé, shape a piece of cardboard, removing narrow strips as follows.   ▣▷▷▷▣
Hold the cardboard above the canapé and shake
paprika, over it; the result will be lines of red in a
pattern, on the canapé.

Parsley, minced or sprigs

Peppers, red and green, cut any shape, often in thin
ribbonlike strips. For Christmas cut tiny stars with
a truffle cutter.

Pickles cut in fancy shapes. To make pickle fans, cut
small gherkins in halves vertically, then cut each
half into vertical sections to within a short space of
the end and spread them apart like a fan.

Pimiento, minced or shaped. Often petal shapes are
fashioned into a flower design with centers of stiff
mayonnaise or of egg yolk.

Radishes, shaped or sliced. A radish rose in the center
of sprigs of cress is effective.

Shrimp

Smoked Salmon, cut in rounds or strips

Truffles, chopped or cut with truffle cutters

Watercress

Chopped pimiento, parsley and hard-boiled egg tossed
together make an effective garnish for some things.

A small pastry bag and a few pastry tubes are invaluable for decorating, also truffle cutters of different designs.

ACCOMPANIMENTS FOR HORS D'OEUVRE

Beaten Biscuits
Cheese Popcorn
Cheese Straws
Melba Toast
Parmesan Cheese Sticks (p. 113)
Popcorn
Potato Chips
Potato Sticks
Potatoes, Julienne
Potatoes, Shoestring
Pretzel Sticks
Ry-Krisp
Salted Nuts
Various Cocktail Biscuits (for sale by the best grocers)

III

FLAVORED BUTTERS

FLAVORED butters are made by first selecting the best dairy butter obtainable. Chefs prefer the fresh unsalted variety. Cream the butter slightly and add the ingredient to give the desired flavor or color, or both.

To prepare the base of seasoned butter rub the yolk of a hard-boiled egg through a fine sieve, cream three or four ounces of butter and combine thoroughly, adding the seasoning desired. Add one or two drops of vegetable coloring to give the right tint, but use sparingly. The egg yolk will help to take up the moisture in the butter and will enable it to stand up better for garnishing purposes and also against the heat of the room. Watch out for the seasoning, however, as the egg detracts from the flavor.

These butters may be used as spreads or for decorating. For the latter, place the butter in a cornucopia made of brown wrapping paper, tapering the end to a very fine point. Use to pipe around the edges of canapés and also to make dots here and there, or you may insert in the paper small icing tubes to make rosettes and leaves. The work must be neatly and artistically done. Acids should be worked in very slowly by the following method: soften butter in a small bowl till the consistency of mayonnaise, then place the bowl in a pan of cracked ice and whip in the liquid very slowly, beating vigorously. The liquid will be taken up through whipping and the mixture become quite light and fluffy.

The yolk of egg is not always given in the following recipes; it may be used or not as wished.

Anchovy Butter

Blend two tablespoons of butter and one-half teaspoon of anchovy paste.

Cheese Butter

Combine equal parts of creamed butter and soft, snappy cheese.

Chive Butter

Add three tablespoons of finely chopped chives and one teaspoon of lemon juice to one-fourth cup of creamed butter.

Cress Butter

Wash cress, dry and remove leaves and chop them. Cream one-half cup of butter and work into it as much cress as it will take up. Season with salt. A little mayonnaise may be added for flavor, or lemon juice and Worcestershire sauce to taste. Another method is to strip the leaves, dry well and mince as fine as possible; then work into the leaves as much butter as they will take up, adding salt and white pepper to season.

Curry Butter

Cream one-half cup of butter and add sufficient curry powder to season well. As curry varies in strength the exact quantity cannot be given.

Green Pepper Butter

Drop two small green peppers into hot fat for one minute. Wipe off the outer skin, cut off the tops, remove the seeds and chop the peppers very fine. Drain well and add to one-fourth cup of creamed butter. Season with salt and lemon juice. Another method is to cut peppers in halves, remove seeds, parboil slightly in water to which a pinch of soda has been added, dry well and use.

Green Savory Butter

Press three tablespoons of cold, cooked spinach through a very fine sieve. Add two tablespoons of butter, two fillets of anchovy, one teaspoon of capers, with paprika and salt to taste. Pound these ingredients until smoothly blended and press all through the sieve.

A color effect can be secured with less work by adding a green color paste to creamed butter which has been highly seasoned.

Horse-radish Butter

Cream six tablespoons of butter, add three to four tablespoons of grated, fresh horse-radish root and season with salt and lemon juice.

Mustard Butter

One teaspoon of dry mustard mixed with spiced vinegar (vinegar remaining from pickles) to a paste. Then whip the paste into four ounces of softened butter, keeping the dish in a pan of ice.

Parsley Butter

Cream one-fourth cup of butter and add one tablespoon of finely chopped parsley and one-half teaspoon of lemon juice with salt to taste.

Pimiento Butter

Wash two or three bright red pimientos and dry thoroughly. As pimientos contain a large percentage of water, after draining squeeze them dry in cheesecloth and then rub through a fine sieve. Add them to one-fourth cup of creamed butter with salt and lemon juice to season, and if wishing more color add one-half teaspoon of paprika. The color will be intensified if the paprika is moistened slightly with a dash of white wine. A little sifted egg yolk added to this butter makes the mixture easier to handle.

Red Butter

Lobster coral pounded smooth, then rubbed through a fine sieve and combined with creamed butter, — or a can of Italian Tomato Paste boiled down with a clove of garlic and a few spices to a point of evaporation, then sieved and added to butter, — gives color and flavor. As coral is not always available, pimientos may be substituted for color.

Savory Butter I

½ cup sweet butter	¼ teaspoon salt
½ teaspoon mustard	¼ teaspoon white pepper
1 teaspoon white vinegar	2 tablespoons olive oil
¼ teaspoon Worcestershire sauce	

Cream the butter and add remaining ingredients. This recipe was given by a chef who said the olive oil in the rule was used to prevent the mixture from becoming too hard when placed in the refrigerator.

Savory Butter II

½ cup sweet butter	Few drops of tarragon vinegar
1 teaspoon dry mustard	
1 teaspoon curry powder	Salt to season
A dash of Tabasco	Yolk of a hard-boiled egg

Cream the butter and blend in the seasonings; then add the egg yolk forced through a sieve and beat until perfectly smooth.

Tomato Catsup Butter

Cream two tablespoons of butter and whip into it two tablespoons of tomato catsup and one teaspoon of lemon juice. Here again one should keep the bowl in cracked ice and add both catsup and acid slowly.

Vegex or Maggi

Either Vegex or Maggi's Seasoning added to cream cheese makes a very good basic spread.

Yellow Butter

Cooked and sifted egg yolk is used to obtain a yellow butter when not using color pastes, but it should be highly seasoned, using mustard for some combinations and curry, yellow cheese or grated fresh horse-radish root for others.

IV

CANAPÉS FOR COCKTAILS

Fish

Anchovy Canapés I
Anchovy Canapés II
Caviar Canapés I
Caviar Canapés II
Caviar Canapés III
Caviar Canapés IV
Caviar Canapés (Russell)
Caviar Canapés (Russian)
Caviar and Anchovy Canapés
Caviar and Cress Sandwiches
Caviar and Tomato Canapés
Caviar Bits
Caviar Fishes
Caviar Latticed Canapés
Crab Meat Canapés
Finnan Haddie Canapés
Fish Mousse Croutons
Herring Canapés I
Herring Canapés II
Lobster Canapés I
Lobster Canapés II
Lobster Canapés, Curried (hot)
Lobster Canapés, Pickled
Lobster Medallions
Sardine Canapés I
Sardine Canapés II (hot)
Sardine Canapés III
Sardine Canapés IV
Sardine Canapés V
Sardine Canapés VI
Sardine and Olive Canapés
Sardine Ovals

Sardines, Broiled (hot)
Shrimp Canapés
Shrimp Canapés Indienne
(hot)
Shrimp and Cress
Canapés
Smoked Salmon
Canapés I
Smoked Salmon
Canapés II
Smoked Salmon Canapés,
Danish
Smoked Salmon and
Cream Cheese Canapés
Smoked Salmon, Caviar
and Anchovy Canapés

FISH

Anchovy Canapés I

Spread anchovy butter on rounds of fried bread and on the outside edge arrange a border of the smallest-sized pearl onions. Set a curled anchovy in the center and in the center of the anchovy pipe a rosette of green or of red butter, using pastry bag and tube.

Anchovy Canapés II

Spread seasoned cream cheese on very small triangles of fried bread and set a curled anchovy in the center of each. Then, using bag and tube, force green butter in the form of leaves around the anchovy or use a few small parsley leaves. Place a dot of pimiento in center of anchovy.

Caviar Canapés I

Slice bread and shape with a six-scalloped cutter. Fry the shapes, drain well and spread with anchovy paste or with cream cheese. Pipe green butter rosettes on each scallop, using bag and tube. Cover the center with seasoned caviar and set three dots of pimiento on that.

Caviar Canapés II

Prepare bread as for the above canapé and spread with savory butter. Make rosettes of green butter on the scallops and place caviar in the center to form a bunch of grapes. Add a small leaf and stem of parsley or make the leaf and stem with green butter.

Caviar Canapés III

Cut bread in rounds and toast until crisp. Spread each round with seasoned caviar and over that sprinkle sifted yolk of hard-boiled egg. On the outside edge set three slices from a pimiento-stuffed olive, arranging them at equal distance from each other.

Caviar Canapés IV

Season caviar with lemon juice and cayenne, spread on cuts of toast and sprinkle with pearl onions.

Caviar Canapés (Russell)

Sauté circular pieces of bread in olive oil and spread with caviar seasoned with cayenne and lemon juice. Set a circle or ring of very thinly sliced Bermuda onion on the outer edge, choosing a ring of onion which has the same circumference as the bread. Place an anchovy ball in the center of each canapé.

Anchovy Balls. Mash the yolks of two hard-boiled eggs and season with anchovy paste, Worcestershire sauce and cayenne. Make into balls with the butter paddles and sprinkle lightly with chopped parsley. Two yolks will yield five balls.

Caviar Canapés (Russian)

Cut bread in half-inch slices and shape with a circular cutter. Score one-third inch from the edge and remove part of the center. Sauté in olive oil and fill with caviar. Pipe green butter on the edge, using bag and small tube, and dot the butter with pearl onions. Sift cooked egg yolk over the caviar.

Caviar and Anchovy Canapés

Prepare a round of fried bread the size of a slice of egg and spread with anchovy butter. On the bread place a ring of egg white sliced from a hard-boiled egg and fill the center with seasoned caviar. Dot the center with a rosette of green butter.

Caviar and Cress Sandwiches

Cut thinly sliced bread into small ovals and spread half of the pieces with seasoned caviar. Spread an equal number of pieces rather thickly with cress butter and put together in pairs. The bread may be toasted on one side if wished.

Caviar and Tomato Canapés

Spread a small round of fried bread with savory butter. Cut slices of tomato measuring the same diameter as the bread and remove the soft part of the slices, leaving distinct sections. Lay the tomato on the bread and fill the sections with seasoned caviar.

Caviar Bits

Cut hot buttered toast into one-half-inch squares. Season caviar with cayenne, lemon juice and, if liked, a slight scraping of onion. Place a bit of caviar on the toast and cover with a spot of whipped cream.

Caviar Fishes

Select small fish molds measuring about two and one-half inches in length. Place a mold upon a thin slice of bread and cut around it. This will give a satisfactory fish shape. Sauté the bread and pipe on each piece a border of yellow butter, then fill in the space with seasoned caviar. Another method is to line the molds with a thin layer of aspic, spread a layer of caviar and finish with aspic. When firm invert the jellied forms on fish shapes of fried bread.

Caviar Latticed Canapés

Shape thin slices of bread with an oval cutter and sauté in olive oil. Chop some onion very fine, moisten with French dressing and spread upon the bread. Over the onion spread seasoned caviar and cover that with sifted egg yolk. Garnish the top with very fine strips of pimiento interlaced as in trelliswork.

Crab Meat Canapés

Spread cuts of toast with red butter and over it lay flakes of crab meat (or salmon) and sprinkle with capers or chopped gherkins.

Finnan Haddie Canapés

One may use either boiled, broiled or canned finnan haddie; break it into small flakes, watching out for small bones. To one cup of flaked fish add about one-third cup of chopped, pimiento-stuffed olives, then moisten to spreading consistency with either mayonnaise or Sauce Tartare. Spread this paste on finger-shaped cuts of fried bread, place a slice of stuffed olive on each end and a leaf of parsley in the center.

Fish Mousse Croutons

Remove skin and bones from about three fourths of a pound of very fresh halibut and force the fish through a purée sieve; there should be one cup. Work slowly and alternately into this the unbeaten whites of two eggs and three-fourths cup of heavy cream. Season with salt and pepper and again force through the sieve.

Poach a small amount in hot water to determine the

texture. If too firm, add more cream; if not firm enough, add more egg white.

Add to this forcemeat small cuts of truffle and of pimiento, also green pepper if wished. Butter small timbale molds, fill with the prepared forcemeat, set them in a pan of hot water and bake in a moderate oven until firm to the touch. When cold, cut in thin slices and place on sautéed rounds of bread, first spreading the rounds lightly with mayonnaise dressing.

Herring Canapés I

Cut sliced bread into finger shapes and toast very crisp. Spread lightly with butter and prepare some very finely minced celery. Press the toast, butter side down, into the celery and enough should adhere to season the canapé. Over the celery place a small square of kippered herring, neatly trimmed, and sprinkle with paprika and minced parsley.

Herring Canapés II

Chop a young cucumber, having small seeds, very fine and drain thoroughly; combine with the same amount of mashed kippered herring and season with minced chives and a dash of vinegar; or one may use half as much cucumber as herring, measured after squeezing in cheesecloth. Spread on cuts of toast and garnish with strips of pimiento.

Lobster Canapés I

Chop lobster meat very fine and season with salt, pepper, lemon juice, olive oil and Tabasco sauce; these should moisten the lobster enough to spread easily as well as to season it. Spread on cuts of bread toasted on one side only and garnish with pickled walnuts and paprika. Shrimp may be prepared in the same way.

Lobster Canapés II

Cut slices of bread in two-inch rounds and sauté in olive oil. Soften finely chopped, well-seasoned lobster meat to a paste with creamed butter and Worcestershire sauce. Make mounds of this mixture on the sautéed bread. Sprinkle sifted lobster coral or paprika over the mound. Then cut olives in crescent-shaped slices and place five of them on each canapé to form a pinwheel.

Curried Lobster Canapés (Hot)

Put into an omelet pan two tablespoons of butter and when melted add two teaspoons of chopped onion and two tablespoons of chopped cress leaves. Let cook in the butter without getting brown and add two teaspoons of flour mixed with one teaspoon of curry. When well blended add half a cup of lobster meat. Cut bread in pieces about one and one-quarter inches wide and two and one-half inches long. Sauté in olive oil. Spread these crusts with the hot lobster mixture and place three tiny strips of pimiento across, diagonally.

Pickled Lobster Canapés

Chop half a cup of lobster meat with two of the large outer leaves from a head of lettuce until both are finely shredded. Season highly with vinegar, salt, dry mustard and black pepper. Set away on ice to become very cold and well blended. Drain, cover rounds of bread, which have been toasted on one side only, with the mixture, and garnish with a section of English Pickled Walnut.

Lobster Medallions

6 small rounds of bread	½ tablespoon gelatin
Olive oil	1½ tablespoons cold water
⅔ cup chopped lobster meat	⅔ cup mayonnaise
Lemon juice	Yolk of a hard-boiled egg
Tabasco and salt	Paprika

From slices of bread cut rounds about the size of a silver dollar and sauté in olive oil. Season the chopped lobster meat very highly and mound on the fried bread to form a half sphere. Place these on a cake rack set over a plate.

Soften gelatin in cold water, set the dish in hot water, stir until dissolved and then add carefully to the mayonnaise. Pour this over the small mounds, letting it run off as it will. This gives a smooth coating which cannot be obtained by spreading with a knife.

Sprinkle the sides with sifted yolk of a hard-boiled egg and shake paprika over the top. Chill and, when perfectly firm, trim the edges.

Sardine Canapés I

Fry small rounds of bread and spread with a fish paste, either sardine, smoked herring or anchovy, mixed with the chopped yolk of a hard-boiled egg. Place a border of chopped egg white around the edge and in the center set a slice of radish. If the radish is scored with a fluted knife it will be more decorative; or a slice of stuffed olive may be used.

Sardine Canapés II (Hot)

Remove all the center from thin slices of small tomatoes. Place the rings thus formed on rounds of fried bread of the same size. Fill the centers with sardines broken in small pieces and seasoned with lemon juice. Heat in the oven before serving.

Sardine Canapés III

Cut teardrop shapes from slices of bread and fry in deep fat. Spread them with sardine butter, sprinkle sifted egg yolk across the tops and then lay on each one a small half gherkin cut fan-shape.

Sardine Canapés IV

Use the same shape as in the preceding recipe and the same spread, or really any one preferred; lay across each canapé five thin strips of ripe olive and place between each two strips a tiny dot of pimiento.

Sardine Canapés V

Spread sardine butter on toasted wafers and dot over with capers or tiny diamonds cut from sour gherkins.

Sardine Canapés VI

Spread potato chips with mashed sardines mixed with lemon juice, mayonnaise and Worcestershire sauce.

Sardine and Olive Canapés

Mix one box of Norwegian sardines with four tablespoons of melted butter; mash them fine and force through a sieve. Blend one-fourth cup of cream into the mixture and spread on fancy cuts of toast. Garnish with both green and ripe olives.

Sardine Ovals

Sardine paste	2 green peppers
Bread	2 pimientos
Olive oil	A few capers
A few pearl onions	

Make a highly seasoned paste of mashed sardines, creamed butter, lemon juice and Tabasco. Sauté oval cuts of bread. Mound the paste on the bread and lay across it, lengthwise, two threadlike strips of pimiento and two of green pepper. Between the strips strew a few capers and pearl onions. Ham paste may be used in place of sardine. The green pepper should be parboiled slightly in water with a pinch of soda to insure a good color and also flexibility.

Broiled Sardines (Hot)

Cut bread in finger-shaped pieces just a bit larger than the sardines. Toast lightly and spread with butter creamed with a little lemon juice. Place the pieces of toast one on another and keep covered in a warm place until the sardines are prepared. Select large, boneless sardines and broil over coals. Place one on each piece of toast and garnish with a section of lemon sprinkled with chopped parsley.

Shrimp Canapés

Spread rounds or ovals of toast with a shrimp purée mixed with mayonnaise and place in the center either a whole shrimp with a spot of caviar on it or a cut of pickled walnut or of ripe olive.

Shrimp Canapés Indienne (Hot)

Spread rounds of fried bread with chutney and set in the center of each a shrimp which has been sautéed in butter with a dash of curry. Place a cress tip or parsley leaf in the center of the shrimp.

Shrimp and Cress Canapés

Spread cuts of toast with cress butter, place a whole shrimp in the center and a spot of tomato catsup in center of the shrimp. The canapé may be made more decorative by piping cress butter around the edge.

Smoked Salmon Canapés I

Toast or fry finger-shaped cuts of bread and place on each a thin slice of smoked salmon of the same size. Pipe mustard butter lengthwise through the center and garnish the butter with three capers.

Smoked Salmon Canapés II

Pound two ounces of smoked salmon with the yolk of a hard-boiled egg, a fillet of anchovy, two ounces of butter and a dash of cayenne. Force the mixture through a sieve and spread on cuts of toast.

Smoked Salmon Canapés (Danish)

Mix four tablespoons of creamed butter with four tablespoons of grated, fresh horse-radish root. Cut graham bread in thin slices, toast, and then cut in domino-shaped pieces. Spread these with the horse-radish butter, and over that lay two very narrow strips of smoked salmon lengthwise and two across. Place three capers lengthwise, one in each center square made by the salmon, and on the long outer edges place a border of chopped parsley.

Smoked Salmon and Cream Cheese Canapés

Place a ring of smoked salmon on rounds of sautéed bread and fill the center with highly seasoned cream cheese; "1812" Wine Sauce is very good or one may use sherry to season the cheese.

Smoked Salmon, Caviar and Anchovy Canapés

Prepare finger-shaped cuts of toast and place a thin slice of smoked salmon at one end and an anchovy fillet at the opposite end with a band of caviar through the center. Add a parsley leaf for garnish.

CANAPÉS FOR COCKTAILS

Meat

Bacon and Cheese Canapés (hot)
Bacon and Peanut Butter Canapés (hot)
Bacon and Tomato Canapés I
Bacon and Tomato Canapés II
Chicken Canapés
Chicken Canapés, Curried
Chicken and Ham Canapés (hot)
Chicken Salad Canapés
Ham and Mushroom Crusts (hot)
Ham and Mustard Canapés
Ham and Ripe Olive Canapés
Ham Canapés, Deviled
Ham, Chicken Liver and Mushroom Canapés
Ham Medallions (hot)

Ham, Mushroom and Cream Cheese Canapés
Liver Canapés, Calves'
Liver Canapés, Chicken or Calves'
Liver Canapés, Chicken, I
Liver Canapés, Chicken, II
Liver Canapés, Chicken, III (Holiday)
Meat Paste Canapés
Pâté de Foie Gras Canapés I
Pâté de Foie Gras Canapés II
Pâté de Foie Gras Canapés III
Pâté de Foie Gras Canapés IV
Sweetbread Canapés (hot)

MEAT

Bacon and Cheese Canapés (Hot)

The ingredients are plain dairy cheese, not too mild, bacon, green pepper and bread.

Force the cheese through the meat chopper together with one-fourth its amount of uncooked bacon and sufficient green pepper for seasoning. Blend evenly and add salt if necessary; the amount will depend upon the saltiness of the bacon and cheese used. Slice bread about one-third inch thick and remove crusts. Spread the mixture rather thickly on the slices of bread, then cut in finger-shaped lengths, place on baking sheet and cook in a very hot oven until well browned and the bread is crisp. These are easy to make and can be made ready except for the baking quite some time before serving.

Bacon and Peanut Butter Canapés (Hot)

2 green peppers	½ loaf bread
2 pimientos	¼ cup butter
½ pound bacon	¼ cup peanut butter
	Cress

Cut green peppers in halves lengthwise, remove seeds and parboil slightly in water to which is added a bit of soda. Cool, and with a truffle cutter stamp out small stars. Cut stars also from the pimiento.

Grill the bacon quite crisp and chop fine. Cut the bread in eighth-inch slices, remove crusts and cut in finger-shaped pieces. Toast these on one side only and spread the untoasted side lightly with the two butters creamed together and salted. Press the spread side of the bread on the chopped bacon and enough will adhere to season well. Place the strips on a baking sheet and set in oven to become very hot. Remove and press a red star in the center and a green star at the ends of each strip. Serve with a garnish of cress.

Bacon and Tomato Canapés I

Cut slices of bread with a round cutter and sauté in olive oil. Spread each one with chopped, fried bacon mixed with a small amount of mayonnaise. On top of that lay slices of tomato, of the same diameter as the bread, which have been marinated a few hours in a French dressing made with strong measures of mustard and sugar. Garnish the tomato with olive sections and chopped, hard-boiled egg.

Bacon and Tomato Canapés II

Cut two rounds of bread for each canapé, removing a small circle of bread from every other slice. Sauté the bread and spread the bottom rounds with horse-radish butter; lay on this a thin slice of tomato of the same circumference. Place the upper slice and fill the space with chopped grilled bacon.

Chicken Canapés

Prepare a mixture of cold cooked chicken, forced through the meat chopper, and *pâté de foie gras,* flavoring with sherry; or to one cup of white meat of chicken add one-fourth cup of sautéed liver and force both through the meat chopper, using the same seasoning. Spread on cuts of toast or fried bread and garnish the top with a shake of paprika and a section of pickled walnut.

Curried Chicken Canapés

Force the white meat from a cooked chicken or fowl through the finest knife of the meat chopper, twice. Moisten it with some heavy cream and some chicken stock and season with salt, white pepper and lemon juice. Spread the mixture on cuts of fried bread and garnish, using pimientos cut into small petal shapes with stems and leaves of green pepper.

Chicken and Ham Canapés (Hot)

Chop a few spoonfuls of cold cooked chicken, and also the same amount of cooked ham, and moisten to a paste with creamed butter. Spread this on fancy cuts of sautéed bread. Cover with grated cheese and run under the gas flame to heat and to melt the cheese. Garnish with olive sections.

Chicken Salad Canapés

Use oval-shaped pieces of thin, buttered toast, also a chicken salad very, very finely minced. Place a scant teaspoon of the salad on each cut of toast. Pipe a narrow border of green butter around the edge and over the top sprinkle two or three shreds of lean, cooked ham (or fine strips of green pepper); or use crisply fried bacon. Capers and paprika are another garnish for this canapé. Serve very cold.

Ham and Mushroom Crusts (Hot)

Cut bread in rather thin slices and shape into pieces three inches long and one and one-half inches wide. Sauté these in olive oil. Moisten finely chopped, cooked ham with highly seasoned brown sauce and spread over the crusts. Over this sprinkle sifted egg yolk and on the top place three small mushroom caps which have been sautéed in butter. Set into the oven a moment to insure the proper temperature. Garnish each service with two sprigs of parsley, either fried or fresh.

Ham and Mustard Canapés

Moisten chopped boiled ham with Bahamian mustard and spread on sautéed cuts of bread. Place thin slices of crisp radish over the top.

Ham and Ripe Olive Canapés

Mix equal amounts of chopped cooked ham and chopped ripe olives, season with mayonnaise and spread on finger-shaped pieces of sautéed dark bread. Lay three cress leaves lengthwise through the center, or use very small celery leaves.

Deviled Ham Canapés

Prepare small rounds of sautéed bread, spread with finely chopped and seasoned ham or a deviled ham preparation, and sprinkle over the top a mixture of chopped white and coarsely sifted yolk of hard-boiled egg, finely chopped parsley and pimiento, the latter well dried before chopping. In the center set a small smooth section of pickled English walnut.

Ham, Chicken Liver and Mushroom Canapés (Hot)

Chop uncooked chicken livers, very fine; there should be one-fourth cup. Fry in a little butter with one tablespoon of chopped onion. When the onion is cooked add two tablespoons of finely chopped, cooked ham and two tablespoons of chopped mushrooms.

When well cooked, bind with a small amount of brown sauce and season to taste with salt and cayenne. Spread the mixture thickly on rounds of sautéed bread, sift egg yolk over the whole, and in the center place a circle of chopped egg white and a sprig of parsley. Serve very hot. Makes six canapés.

Ham Medallions (Hot)

Cut thin slices from cold boiled ham and for twelve servings stamp out twenty-four rounds about one and one-half inches in diameter. Spread half of the rounds with prepared mustard, sprinkle with brown sugar and cover with remaining rounds. Bake in a moderate oven until sugar and mustard are well melted, then serve on rounds of fried bread of the same size.

Ham, Mushroom and Cream Cheese Canapés

Chop mushrooms and sauté in butter. Work a cream cheese until smooth and then blend enough of the cheese into the mushrooms just to hold them together; season highly and add a few spoonfuls of chopped boiled ham. Spread on fancy cuts of sautéed bread and garnish with chopped parsley and paprika.

Calves' Liver Canapés

Sauté liver and chop fine, then add chopped crisp bacon and moisten to spreading consistency with sherry. Spread this mixture on sautéed rounds of bread and cover with a doughnut-shaped slice of bread, also

TRAY SERVICE OF COCKTAIL CANAPÉS

Reading down: Pâté de Foie Gras Canapés II — Caviar Canapés II —
Sardine Ovals — Caviar Canapés I — Tomato Canapés

INDIVIDUAL COCKTAIL TRAY
FOR BRIDGE SERVICE

sautéed. Place in the open space a small tip of celery or half of a stuffed olive.

Liver Canapés, Chicken or Calves'

Force cooked liver through the meat chopper and while hot add a little butter, dash of onion juice and salt and pepper to season. Spread cuts of fried bread with savory butter and then the prepared liver. Sprinkle minced parsley around the edge and sifted egg yolk in the center.

Chicken Liver Canapés I

Cook chicken livers and work to a paste with enough butter to soften, add a little heavy cream and sherry, salt and pepper to taste. Spread the paste quite thickly on cuts of fried bread, sprinkle with paprika and in the center set a very small pickled onion.

Chicken Liver Canapés II

Sauté chicken livers, chop them and add a little chopped onion. Crush all with a fork, season and spread on toasted rye bread.

Chicken Liver Canapés III (Holiday)

Sauté rounds of bread and spread with a paste made of chicken livers and chopped cooked ham. Cut a green pepper, remove seeds and parboil in water with a pinch of baking soda, cool and chop quite fine. Sprinkle the pepper over the paste thicker on the outside edge than in the center. Select small radishes, cut them across in halves, then cut each half vertically into thin slices; arrange these in the center of the canapé with the red edge uppermost.

Meat Paste Canapés

Mix any ground, cooked meat with Italian Tomato Paste to moisten and use as a spread on sautéed bread; cover with a thin layer of cream cheese highly seasoned with curry powder and sprinkle with paprika.

Pâté de Foie Gras *Canapés I*

Sauté rounds of white bread and spread with *pâté de foie gras* purée, or use any of the liver spreads given; cover with a slice of tomato which has been spread lightly with mayonnaise and garnish with half a stuffed olive in which a tiny tip of cress has been inserted.

Pâté de Foie Gras *Canapés II*

Spread scalloped rounds of bread which have been sautéed in olive oil with *pâté de foie gras* and cover that with chopped tomato aspic. Arrange over that two groups of ripe olive crescents and two groups of green olive crescents. Fill the space between the green olives with sifted egg yolk and between the ripe olives with chopped egg white. The canapé is just as delicious without the egg and much less work.

Pâté de Foie Gras *Canapés III*

Sauté finger-shaped pieces of bread and spread them with *pâté de foie gras* purée combined with the firm part of a tomato cut small. Cut a small slice from a ripe olive to give a rounded top surface and place in the center of the canapé. At each end lay a threadlike strip of pimiento to form a letter "S"; then at the base of the olive arrange three tiny leaves of parsley.

Pâté de Foie Gras *Canapés IV*

Sauté round cuts of bread, spread them with *pâté de foie gras* purée and over that set a round of highly seasoned tomato jelly which was molded in a thin sheet and stamped out with the same cutter that was used for the bread.

Sweetbread Canapés (Hot)

Mash one ounce of Roquefort cheese (or Parmesan) and add one-third teaspoon of dry mustard and one-half teaspoon of curry; then add one-half teaspoon of Worcestershire sauce and, last, six tablespoons of creamed butter. Spread this mixture on thin slices of sautéed bread and cover with thin slices of a sweetbread which has been parboiled. Mix a very little heavy cream with some grated Parmesan cheese, spread it sparingly over the sweetbread and brown in a hot oven.

CANAPÉS FOR COCKTAILS

Cheese

Cheese and Almond Canapés (hot)
Cheese and Chive Canapés
Cheese and Nut Canapés
Cheese and Olive Canapés I (hot)
Cheese and Olive Canapés II
Cheese and Pimiento Canapés (hot)
Cheese Daisies
Cheesehill Wafers
Gruyère Croutons (hot)
Lucerne Canapés
Roquefort Wafers
Savory Cheese Rusks (hot)
Spanish Canapés
Volendam Canapés I
Volendam Canapés II

CHEESE

Cheese and Almond Canapés (Hot)

Blanch, chop and sauté almonds to measure three tablespoons and mix with six tablespoons of grated Parmesan cheese, three tablespoons of heavy cream, three tablespoons of minced parsley and salt and pepper to taste. Spread this mixture on cuts of sautéed bread, sprinkle with additional chopped and browned almonds and heat thoroughly.

Cheese and Chive Canapés

6 slices of bread
Olive oil
1 cup cream cheese
3 teaspoons chives

A little mayonnaise
2 small tomatoes
Melted butter, about two tea-
    spoons
Paprika

Cut bread in rounds two inches in diameter and sauté in olive oil until crisp. Combine one half of the cheese with the chives finely chopped and mayonnaise to season. Spread the bread very thinly with this mixture, then place on that a thin slice of tomato of the same diameter. Spread the slice of tomato with the seasoned cheese and sprinkle with paprika. Add melted butter to the remaining cheese, enough to season well, and pipe a border on each tomato, using a small icing tube and pastry bag or paper cornet.

Cheese and Nut Canapés

Season cream cheese very highly, make into a roll of the same diameter as the crackers to be used (about one and one-half inches) and roll in chopped pecan nut meats or chopped salted almonds. Chill, then slice and lay on crackers.

Cheese and Olive Canapés I (Hot)

Prepare finger-shaped pieces of dark bread and toast them. Spread each one with cream cheese and sprinkle with chopped olives and very coarsely grated yellow cheese, preferably Edam, although Young America may be used. Place on a baking sheet and set in the oven until the cheese melts and all is well heated.

Cheese and Olive Canapés II

Cut bread in one-fourth-inch slices and shape in rectangular pieces about two by three inches. Cut a small piece diagonally off each corner. Toast the bread lightly on one side only. Spread the untoasted side with highly seasoned cheese butter, sprinkle with paprika and on the outer edges place a border of finely chopped olives.

Cheese and Pimiento Canapés

Cut bread in oval or finger shapes and sauté. Place on the bread a slice of cheese cut in the same shape and over that a slice of pimiento which has been well dried and shaped. Place on a baking sheet in a hot oven until the cheese melts, then sprinkle the pimiento with minced parsley.

Cheese Daisies

Sauté small rounds of bread and spread them with highly seasoned cream cheese. Cut thin slices from Young America cheese and stamp out rounds with a small cutter measuring one inch in diameter. Using the same cutter place a section of it on the edge of the round to cut an oval-shaped piece. The round will yield three of these petal-shaped pieces with little waste — just a small spot in the center.

Place five of these petals, radiating from the center,

on each round of prepared bread and finish with a
small round piece of ripe olive placed in the center.

Cheesehill Wafers

Season cream cheese, moisten slightly with cream
and force through pastry bag and star tube on round
thin wafers. Press half of a small pimiento-stuffed olive
into the center of each mound of cheese. One may vary
this wafer by using a small round of watermelon pickle
instead of the olive.

Gruyère Croutons (Hot)

Cut bread in oval shapes and toast on one side only.
Mix one cup of grated Gruyère cheese with salt and
paprika to taste and cook for only a second in a small
amount of heavy cream, about three tablespoons, and
one tablespoon of butter, just enough to form a paste.
Spread this paste on the untoasted side of the bread
and bake until piping hot. Sprinkle with paprika.

Lucerne Canapés

2 tinfoil portions of soft
  Gruyère cheese
About 4 tablespoons of
  mayonnaise

½ cup coarsely chopped
  ripe olives
Tabasco and salt

Rub the cheese through a sieve; there should be one-
half cup. Mix with the mayonnaise, fold in the olives
and season to taste. Spread on cuts of toast or sautéed
bread and sprinkle with paprika.

Roquefort Wafers

Make a paste of one tablespoon of Roquefort cheese, two teaspoons of olive oil, one-half teaspoon of mustard, one-fourth teaspoon of Worcestershire and six shakes of cayenne pepper. Spread the mixture on long narrow wafers and garnish the top of each with sections of ripe olives.

Savory Cheese Rusks (Hot)

¾ cup grated cheese	1 tablespoon mild vinegar
½ teaspoon dry mustard	Worcestershire sauce
1½ tablespoons olive oil	Salt and paprika
1/16 teaspoon baking soda	

Mix all ingredients, seasoning to taste, and beat until creamy. Spread on shapes of bread and brown in a very hot oven.

Spanish Canapés

1½ tablespoons chopped green pepper	Salt and cayenne to taste
1 teaspoon finely chopped onion	1 egg slightly beaten
1 tablespoon butter	2 tablespoons beer or ginger ale
⅓ cup stewed tomato	½ loaf bread
¾ pound Young America cheese	5 ripe olives
	5 green olives

Fry pepper and onion in butter five minutes, stirring constantly; add tomatoes, the cheese sliced thin and seasonings. Stir over a low fire in a shallow pan of considerable surface until the cheese melts; then add the egg and last the beer. Stir till egg is cooked and chill. Spread on finger-shaped pieces of toast. Lay diagonally, over the top of each canapé, sections of green olives and close to them sections of ripe olives, using about three of each to a canapé.

Volendam Canapés I

Make a paste of yellow cheese forced through a sieve and highly seasoned, and mound it upon oval cuts of fried bread, bringing it up to a narrow top like a roof. Place half a stuffed olive in the center of the canapé, or a leaf of parsley.

Volendam Canapés II

Take oval cuts of fried bread, mound highly seasoned cream cheese upon them and sprinkle with paprika. Any seasonings may be worked into the cheese, such as "1812" Wine Sauce or sherry, curry, fresh herbs, etc. These are attractive, because not overdecorated, and arranged with the preceding canapés give a pleasing contrast.

CANAPÉS FOR COCKTAILS

Miscellaneous

Czechoslovak Shells	Radish Canapés
Fan Canapés	Tomato Canapés
Mushroom Fingers (hot)	Valentine Canapés (hot)
Pimiento Stars	Vegetable Canapés

MISCELLANEOUS

Czechoslovak Shells

Brush the inside of tiny shell molds with olive oil and set them in a pan of cracked ice. Place in the bottom of each a small amount of clear tomato aspic; when firm, lay in small bits of ripe olive, pimiento and green pepper, together with antipasto cut small. Set these with aspic and continue until the mold is full. Use only enough aspic to hold these pieces in place. The molds should be filled mostly with the antipasto, with enough of the olive and pepper to give the required color and enough of the aspic to keep the shape. Turn these molds out, when firm, on round cuts of sautéed bread.

Fan Canapés

Cut teardrop shapes from thin slices of bread and sauté in olive oil or in butter. Spread them with Yellow Butter II and sprinkle with paprika. Cut an inch and a half long gherkin into fan shape, the direction for which will be found under "Garnishes." Place the gherkin in the center of the canapé, spreading the cut sections, and between them lay thin strips of pimiento.

Mushroom Fingers (Hot)

Spread finger-shaped pieces of toast with small mushrooms which have been thinly sliced, sautéed in butter and combined with a little thick cream blended with prepared mustard. The flavor is unusual.

A CLOSE-UP OF CANAPÉS

ASSORTED HORS D'OEUVRE

Stuffed Prunes — Sardine Canapés II — Curried Chicken Canapés —
Ham Balls — Chipped Beef Balls

Pimiento Stars

Cut slices of bread into star shapes and sauté in olive oil. Spread with Yellow Butter II and place on each point a piece of pimiento cut to fit the point. In the center pipe a rather good-sized rosette of the butter and place at its base a few tiny parsley leaves.

Radish Canapés

Sauté or toast finger-shaped cuts of bread and spread them with some savory paste or with highly seasoned cream cheese.

Prepare small radishes by scoring them lengthwise with a lemon scorer or with a fluted knife; or, not having either of these, cut out narrow strips with a plain sharp knife. Then cut the radishes crosswise into thin slices and arrange them on the canapés, overlapping one another with a tiny parsley leaf in the center.

Tomato Canapés

Cut rounds from thin slices of bread, toast them and spread with horse-radish butter. Over the butter lay a very thin slice of tomato the same diameter as the bread, season with salt and pepper and, using a star tube, press seasoned cream cheese in the center. Then on each tomato arrange five crescent-shaped sections of ripe olive to resemble a pinwheel, tucking the inner points under the cheese to hold them in place.

Valentine Canapés (Hot)

Cut slices of bread into heart shapes and with the same cutter stamp out hearts from slices of pimiento, first drying them well. Sauté both bread and pimiento in butter or olive oil, lay the pimientos on the bread and sprinkle with salt, pepper and finely minced parsley.

Vegetable Canapés

Sauté finger-shaped pieces of white bread until very crisp and spread with a heavy mayonnaise. Prepare equal amounts of very finely minced cucumber, celery, young raw carrot, pecan nut meats and green pepper which has been parboiled slightly in water containing a pinch of soda. These all should be minced separately and then combined and seasoned with salt, pepper and lemon juice. Spread the vegetables on a dish and press the mayonnaise side of the bread upon them, when enough should adhere to cover the bread. Sprinkle on top one or two pieces of Pickled English Walnut. Set the canapés on a cake cooler over a dish and pour over them an aspic made from canned Madrilène consommé, using four teaspoons of granulated gelatin to one and one-third cups of the liquid. The aspic should be slightly thickened and poured over at just the right moment. Set the canapés in the refrigerator until the aspic is fully set but not long enough for the bread to lose its crispness.

V

PIERCED SAVORIES

Fish

Caviar Blackberries
Finnan Haddie Croquettes
Fish Balls (hot)
Fish Balls Surprise, Bacon (hot)
Fish Balls Surprise, Piccalilli (hot)
Oysters, Fried (hot)
Sardine Cuts (hot)
Scallops and Bacon (hot)
Shrimp, Cold
Shrimp, Deviled (hot)
Smoked Salmon Balls (hot)
Smoked Salmon and Cream Cheese Buds

PIERCED SAVORIES

Pierced savories are those appetizing bits which are impaled on small wooden skewers called picks and are generally inserted in some form such as a grapefruit, melon, eggplant, etc., or in perforated wooden or pottery shapes. Many prefer to have them laid upon serving dishes and in that case pretzel or potato sticks may be substituted for the picks if wished. Another "set-up" is to place them in bonbon cups with skewers uppermost.

FISH

Caviar Blackberries

Season cream cheese with lemon juice and cayenne, make oval shapes like berries, then roll them in well-drained caviar until they look like blackberries. A touch of parsley or cress at the top will add to the appearance. This idea may be carried out with high seasoning for the cheese and chopped ripe olives for the covering.

Finnan Haddie Croquettes

½ cup flaked cooked finnan haddie
Yolk of a hard-boiled egg
Potato chips

2 tablespoons creamed butter
1 teaspoon or more of cream
Seasoning

The finnan haddie may be boiled or broiled, or the canned is satisfactory, but watch out for the small bones. Combine the fish with the butter, the egg yolk sifted, and moisten with cream. Make into croquette shapes about an inch long and roll in crushed potato chips, then skewer. The shapes may be made in advance but should not be rolled in the chips until the last moment as they soften on standing. Be sure to crisp the chips before crushing them.

Fish Balls (*Hot*)

2 heaping cups of potato cut small	½ tablespoon of butter
	⅛ teaspoon white pepper
1 cup of codfish cut in shreds	1 egg
Salt if necessary	

Cook potatoes and fish in boiling water until the potato is done, drain well, mash, add the egg well beaten, seasoning and butter, and beat until feathery light. If the mixture stands until cool it can be handled better than when hot. Use a heaping teaspoon for each ball, which should be about the size of a large olive, and push it off the spoon into the hot fat. Use a frying basket, drain balls well and spear.

Fish Balls Surprise, Bacon (*Hot*)

Take a heaping teaspoon of the fish-ball mixture, make a slight depression in the center, in which place a very small amount of chopped, well-grilled bacon. Cover with the mixture and proceed as in fish balls.

Fish Balls Surprise, Piccalilli (*Hot*)

Prepare as in the preceding recipe, using a small bit of piccalilli well drained and, if in coarse pieces, slightly chopped.

Fried Oysters (*Hot*)

Clean selected oysters and dry thoroughly, season with salt and pepper, dip in flour, beaten egg and then cracker crumbs. Fry in deep fat and drain on clean absorbent paper.

Sardine Cuts (*Hot*)

Spread a slice of entire-wheat bread (crusts removed) with sardine paste and over that a thin layer of cream cheese, like an icing, then roll and enclose the roll in waxed paper. Place in the refrigerator for a few hours to become firm. Slice the roll into inch pieces, lay them on a buttered pan and brown in a 400° to 500° F. oven. Skewer for serving.

Scallops and Bacon (*Hot*)

Clean and dry scallops and wrap with a piece of thinly sliced bacon, skewering it on with a toothpick. Be sure that the bacon overlaps as it shrinks in the baking. Set the wrapped scallops on a rack in the oven until the bacon is well crisped, or broil them if preferred. If the skewers are charred in the cooking remove and insert serving picks. Make a sauce of melted butter, seasoned with lemon juice and Worcestershire sauce, in which to dunk the scallops. The sauce is a very important part of this savory.

Shrimp

Put two shrimp together like a sandwich, using horse-radish butter between them. They may be served in this way or elaborated by coating with aspic. If using aspic garnish the shrimp with tiny cuts of truffle.

Deviled Shrimp (Hot)

Clean the shrimp and spread them with a prepared mustard, dip them in flour, then in slightly beaten egg and last in finely sifted bread crumbs. Sauté in hot butter in an omelet pan and skewer for serving.

Smoked Salmon Balls (Hot)

Soak one and one-half pounds of smoked salmon overnight in water to cover and then cook in fresh water slowly for ten minutes. Melt two tablespoons of butter, add five tablespoons of flour and one cup of chicken stock and cook for five minutes; add two cups of flaked salmon, two pimientos finely chopped, and season to taste. Shape into small balls, roll in flour, then beaten egg, and last in fine bread crumbs. Fry in deep fat, drain well and skewer. This amount makes about forty balls.

Smoked Salmon and Cream Cheese Buds

Season cream cheese with white pepper and spread on neat, thin slices of smoked salmon. Roll, chill and cut in one-inch lengths. Pinch one end closely together and insert pick.

PIERCED SAVORIES

Meat

Bacon and Artichokes (hot)
Bacon and Chicken Livers (hot)

Bacon and Prunes, Baked (hot)
Bacon and Watermelon Pickle (hot)
Bacon Crisps (hot)
Calves' Liver Squares (hot)
Chipped Beef Balls
Ham Balls
Pâté de Foie Gras Acorns
Sausages, Grilled (hot)

MEAT

Bacon and Artichokes (Hot)

Use the very tiny hearts of artichokes which come in bottles and are preserved in oil, and wrap with bacon. Skewer and either broil or bake them until the bacon is crisp. Remove cooking skewer and insert serving pick.

Bacon and Chicken Livers (Hot)

Wrap chicken livers in thinly sliced bacon, skewer and place on a rack in the oven until bacon is crisp and brown. Insert fresh skewers.

Bacon and Prunes, Baked (Hot)

Select large fine prunes, wash them well and steam them until they are soft but not mushy. Remove the stones and fill each space with a small green olive which has been stoned; or remove the center from a stuffed olive. Wrap each prune after stuffing with a thin slice of bacon, fastening it with a pick. Bake in a hot oven until the bacon is crisp, drain on paper, remove cooking skewer and insert serving pick.

Bacon and Watermelon Pickle (Hot)

Cut sections of watermelon pickle into pieces about an inch square and one-half inch thick and dry well. Then wrap each square with a *very* thin slice of bacon to overlap well as it shrinks in the cooking. Insert picks, put on a rack set over a pan and bake. When bacon is done, remove the skewers, which have probably become charred, and insert serving picks.

Bacon Crisps (Hot)

Slice bread, remove crusts and shape into two-inch squares. Spread with peanut butter, roll, and then skewer a small piece of thinly sliced bacon around each roll, having it overlap well, and cut in halves or thirds. Fry in deep fat, drain on absorbent paper and serve on fresh skewers if the first ones become charred.

Calves' Liver Squares (Hot)

Place one-half-inch slices of liver in a shallow plate, sprinkle with baking soda, pour over boiling water, let stand a minute or two and then pour it off. Turn the slice and repeat. Dry well, remove outside skin and all tough, stringy portions, cut into one-inch squares, sprinkle with salt and pepper, dredge well with flour, and fry in deep fat. Drain well and serve on picks.

Chipped Beef Balls

Season cream cheese with Bahamian mustard (a preparation that is spiced) and add chipped beef cut very fine with shears, folding in as much as the cheese will take up. Form into balls or acorn shapes, sprinkle with paprika and skewer. If using acorn shapes insert a parsley leaf in the tip. Substitutes may be chopped ham for the beef and prepared mustard instead of Bahamian. For another variation moisten and season cheese with Bahamian mustard and roll in finely cut chipped beef.

Ham Balls

Take equal amounts of chopped, cold boiled ham and sifted, hard-cooked egg yolks and work into a stiff paste with a little mayonnaise dressing. Season highly with salt and pepper and form into balls an inch in diameter. Stud these balls with a few capers which have been well drained and insert serving picks.

Pâté de Foie Gras *Acorns*

Form *pâté de foie gras* purée into small acorn shapes and roll the tops in chopped truffles. Coat them with thin aspic and chill.

The following paste makes a good substitute for the more expensive preparation. Force through a sieve sautéed chicken livers and cooked white meat of

chicken, using half as much liver as chicken. Moisten
with sherry and season with salt and pepper.

The aspic is not absolutely necessary but makes the
savories more attractive; also one may substitute
chopped ripe olives for truffles.

Grilled Sausages (Hot)

To cook cocktail sausages prick them with a sharp
fork and do not cook at too high a temperature —
about 375° F. Some persons advocate putting a small
amount of water in the pan when first placing them in
the oven, pouring it off when the sausages are half
done.

PIERCED SAVORIES

Cheese

Cheese and Bacon Croquettes
Cheese Balls (hot)
Cheese Balls, Cream
Cheese Balls, East Indian
Cheese Balls, Gruyère
Cheese Footballs
Cheese Snacks
Cheese Truffles
Nut Balls
Pumpernickel Dominoes
Watermelon Pickle and Cream Cheese Cubes

CHEESE

Cheese and Bacon Croquettes

Season cream cheese very highly, using grated, fresh horse-radish root for the predominating flavor. Shape into inch-long croquette forms and roll in finely chopped, well-grilled bacon. Skewer and serve before the bacon softens.

Cheese Balls (*Hot*)

3 tablespoons butter	Unbeaten yolks of two eggs
¼ cup flour	1 cup of cheese
⅔ cup milk	½ cup grated Gruyère cheese

Melt butter, add flour and, when smooth, the milk. Add egg yolks and when blended add the cheese cut in small dice and the grated cheese. When cheese is melted remove from the fire and season with salt and cayenne and chill. Shape into balls, roll in flour, then beaten egg, and last in fine bread crumbs. Fry in deep fat, drain on absorbent paper and skewer for serving.

Cream Cheese Balls

Season cream cheese with "1812" Sauce, shape into balls, roll in chopped salted almonds and skewer.

East Indian Cheese Balls

Season cream cheese with curry powder and chopped chutney and shape into balls. Roll them immediately in chopped browned coconut and place in the refrigerator to chill. Serve on skewers.

Gruyère Cheese Balls

½ cup cream cheese
½ cup grated Gruyère
  cheese

½ cup dextrinized bread
  crumbs
2 tablespoons melted butter

Mix the cream cheese and Gruyère until smooth and make into small balls about the size of a filbert, roll in melted butter and then in crumbs. To make these crumbs, butter two slices of stale bread and place in a moderate oven to become golden brown throughout, then crush, sift and use.

Cheese Footballs

Grate some Gruyère cheese and combine with cream cheese. Season very highly with sherry or with "1812" Sauce, make into balls and press on each one lengthwise five sections of ripe olives cut in crescent shape. Chill and skewer.

Cheese Snacks

Make small balls of cottage cheese mixed with chopped ripe olives, chopped chives, salt, pepper and a little chopped thyme. The dried herb may be used if the fresh one is not available.

Cheese Truffles

Drain pimiento-stuffed olives, small or of medium size, and wrap each one in cream cheese; then roll them in finely chopped pecan nut meats and set in the refrigerator to become well chilled.

Nut Balls

Mash with a fork one half a cream cheese, add one tablespoon of mayonnaise and then four tablespoons of peanut butter. It is better not to have the latter entirely blended. Season with salt and Tabasco and make into small balls. Have ready finely sifted bread crumbs made from unbuttered dextrinized bread and roll the balls in them. Chill until firm and skewer. These balls soften very quickly in a warm room but are especially good.

Pumpernickel Dominoes

Spread two thin slices of pumpernickel with a soft, seasoned yellow cheese and top with a third slice. Press these together firmly and cut into small domino shapes. Thin slices of cold, steamed brown bread may be substituted for the pumpernickel.

Watermelon Pickle and Cream Cheese Cubes

Cut slices of watermelon pickle into small cubes, remove all moisture and spread the top and sides with cream cheese, beaten with a fork to spreading consistency. Decorate with sections of ripe olives, chill and skewer.

PIERCED SAVORIES

Miscellaneous

Avocado Cubes
Cauliflower and Shrimp

Cauliflower Sprigs
Chestnuts, Glazed
Egg Sections, Stuffed
Kumquats, Stuffed
Mushroom Caps, Stuffed
Olives Stuffed with Chicken Salad
Olives Stuffed with *Pâté de Foie Gras*
Olives Stuffed with Spiced Cheese
Onions, Glazed
Prunes and Cream Cheese with Rum Flavor

MISCELLANEOUS

Avocado Cubes

Cut an avocado in halves, remove stone, cut each half in two, then peel and cut the flesh into cubes to make a mouthful. Avocado musses easily so that it must be handled very carefully. Marinate the cubes in a dressing of lime juice, salt and white pepper. Chill well, drain and skewer.

Cauliflower and Shrimp

Separate a head of cooked and chilled cauliflower into sprigs and arrange in a mound with an equal amount of shrimp. These may be speared or the picks placed near at hand. Also, a bowl of Russian dressing in which to dip the pieces should be conveniently near.

Cauliflower Sprigs

Break a head of cooked cauliflower into flowerets of uniform size. Marinate them in French dressing, drain well and roll in dry, finely powdered parsley.

Glazed Chestnuts

Shell chestnuts and boil in salted water for a few minutes, then drain and cook in brown stock until well glazed, brown and tender. To obtain a good glaze, they should cook until the stock is practically absorbed.

Stuffed Egg Sections

Hard-boil the eggs, cool and cut in halves. Remove yolks, mash them and season highly with A 1 sauce, mustard, Worcestershire sauce and tarragon vinegar; or use some of the fillings given under "Stuffed Eggs." Chill thoroughly; then with a sharp knife cut each half into fourths, sprinkle with paprika and serve on picks.

Stuffed Kumquats

Wash the kumquats well, wipe and cut in halves. Remove centers, which consist of tough pith and seeds, and fill with well-seasoned cream cheese.

Stuffed Mushroom Caps (Hot)

Select mushrooms measuring about an inch or an inch and a half across; peel, stem and sauté them in butter until soft. Then place in the center of each a very little creamed chicken cut fine, seasoned with curry or sherry, and run them under the flame for a few minutes.

Olives Stuffed with Chicken Salad

Make a very finely minced chicken salad, adding capers and high seasoning. Use to stuff large green olives which have been stoned, or one may use pimiento olives; remove the center and the olive is ready.

Olives Stuffed with Pâté de Foie Gras

Remove the stones from large green olives and fill in the space with *pâté de foie gras* worked up with sifted yolk of a hard-boiled egg and a little butter; or use the recipe for *pâté de foie gras* acorns made of chicken liver and sherry.

Olives Stuffed with Spiced Cheese

Select mammoth olives both green and black, remove stones and stuff with spiced cheese. The easiest way to fill these is to use a bag and small tube to force the mixture into the olive.

Glazed Onions

Buy the small white pickling onions and peel them. Cook for a few minutes in boiling salted water, drain and place on a cloth to absorb all moisture. Take a shallow pan of considerable surface, as the onions should only cover the bottom of the pan, and melt in it two or three tablespoons of butter; add the same amount of sugar and stir well. Then add the onions and toss them about until well coated with the sugar, which will become caramelized. Salt and pepper them during the cooking. Serve on picks. These are good cold as well as hot.

Prunes and Cream Cheese with Rum Flavor

Wash medium-sized prunes and soak in rum to cover or almost cover, stirring occasionally. It will take twenty-four hours or more for them to become soft enough so that the stones may be removed. Remove the stones and fill the space with cream cheese, bringing the two cut edges together so that no cheese shows.

VI

HORS D'OEUVRE FOR THE COMPARTMENT DISH

MANY of the suggestions given under "Pierced Savories" will be suitable for use in the compartment dish. There are two types of hors d'oeuvre to be used in this classification — those which may be eaten from the fingers and are, comparatively speaking, dry, and those which are very moist and require plate and fork. The latter are more fitting for first-course savories at luncheon.

Dry Savories

Anchovy Balls

Celery, Stuffed

Celery Trees

Cheese Oysterettes

Ham Cornets with Spinach

Iced Vegetables

Olives, Marinated

Olives with Cheese Shreds

Olives with Garlic

Olives with Meat Shreds

Radishes, Stuffed, I

Radishes, Stuffed, II

Stuffed French Roll Slices

DRY SAVORIES

Anchovy Balls

Mash the yolks of two hard-boiled eggs and season with anchovy paste, Worcestershire sauce and cayenne.

Make into balls with butter paddles and sprinkle lightly with chopped parsley. Two yolks will yield five balls.

Stuffed Celery

Select two stalks that fit well together and stuff the groove of each with any preferred filling. Bring the stalks together to make a round treelike stalk and chill. To serve, cut into inch pieces with a very sharp knife and heap in relish dish.

Celery Trees

Select celery stalks with a decided curve so that sufficient filling can be used. Cut the stalks in two and one-half inch lengths, fringe the tops and let stand in ice water for several hours. Remove, wipe thoroughly and fill with a paste made by combining equal parts of dairy and peanut butter seasoned highly with salt, cayenne and a few chopped pimiento-stuffed olives. Put two pieces together to form a round treelike stalk and place in compartment dish. Any filling can be substituted for the one given.

Cheese Oysterettes

Spread oysterettes with Spiced Cheese mixture, sprinkle with paprika, chill and place in dish. These are just a tasty mouthful easy to prepare and to eat.

Ham Cornets with Spinach

Trim thin slices of cold boiled ham into inch-and-a-half squares. Place on each square a teaspoon of highly seasoned and finely chopped spinach. The spinach must be cooked with a pinch of soda to insure a good color, which is most essential here. Then roll into cornucopia shape.

Iced Vegetables

Select from the following salad vegetables a combination that will be appetizing and in season and see that they are served crisp and perfectly chilled: —

Cucumbers cut in lengthwise sections, French endive, sticklike cuts of Chinese cabbage, curled celery or plain if preferred, sections of fennel bulbs, scallions, radishes, peeled or scraped with a green tip left on, new young carrots cut lengthwise very, very thin and allowed to stand in ice water until they curl slightly, and tips of cress.

There should be one or more bowls of dressing to accompany this dish.

Olives Marinated

Put about one-half cup of olive oil into a preserve jar, add two slices of lemon, one clove of garlic cut in fourths and four whole cloves. Drain the liquid from a pint jar of ripe olives (colossal size) and dry the olives on a cloth. Add the olives to the oil, cover the jar tightly and turn it upside down a few times so the olives will be well coated with the oil. Set in the refrigerator overnight. If the olives are slightly pricked with a fork they will absorb more flavor.

Olives with Cheese Shreds

Stone large green olives or if you haven't an olive stoner buy pimiento-stuffed olives and push out the centers. Prepare julienne-like strips about one and one-half inches long of white (dairy) cheese and yellow (Young America) and insert in the space which has been made, having the shreds extend slightly on both ends or place all white cheese in part of the olives and all yellow in the rest.

Olives with Garlic

Mash two cloves of garlic very fine, place twenty-four colossal ripe olives on top and pour over them one cup of olive oil. Stir the olives around in the oil and chill for an hour, then drain.

Olives with Meat Shreds

Prepare olives as for Olives with Cheese Shreds, using, instead of cheese, shreds of ham, chicken or tongue. Both green and ripe olives may be used for contrast.

Stuffed Radishes I

Select good-sized radishes of a round shape rather than long, scrub well and leave a green leaf at the base. Cut a slice from the top and, using a small French knife, remove the center. Fill the space with cream

HORS D'OEUVRE PLATTER

Celery Trees — Olives with Meat Shreds — Chicken Liver Canapés III —
Bacon and Peanut Butter Canapés — Caviar Canapés III —
Cress — Cut Radishes

cheese highly seasoned with chopped chives, salt and white pepper.

Stuffed Radishes II

Select round radishes, scrub, leave a green tip on the end and cut from the top to the stem end into five or six sections, then let stand in ice water until well opened. Season cream cheese, make into balls and press one down into the center of each radish.

Stuffed French Roll Slices

Take crisp French rolls with square ends, cut off the two ends from each and remove the soft center crumb. Then spread as much of the lining as possible with creamed or savory butter. Fill the space solidly with any potted meat or fish paste and chill. When thoroughly cold, slice the rolls and you have circular snacks with crust all around outside and different-colored centers. Each roll will cut into eight or ten slices and it is interesting to use more than one kind of filling.

The fish spread of cream cheese, ripe olive and sardine is very good, and especially so the ham, ripe olive and mayonnaise given under "Canapés." In fact there are many others just as suitable.

Moist Savories

Anchovies with Pimiento Butter
Antipasto

Beets, Stuffed, I
Beets, Stuffed, II
Cabbage Relish

Celery Relish I

Celery Relish II

Chicken Shreds Indienne

Chicken Shreds Mexican

Cucumbers, Wilted

Eggs, Stuffed

   Cress Eggs

   Horse-radish Eggs

   Lobster Eggs

Olive Eggs

Sardine Eggs

Savory Eggs

Smoked Salmon Eggs

Eggs with Mustard Sauce

Lobster Slices

Salad Relish

Shrimp Relish

Sweetbread and Tomatoes

Vanderbilt Shreds

MOIST SAVORIES

Anchovies with Pimiento Butter

Drain pimientos from the can and squeeze in cheese-cloth until quite dry. Then rub through a fine sieve and add enough creamed butter to make a smooth paste. Season with salt. Select the curled anchovies which come in oil in small bottles, lay them on soft paper to absorb the oil and, with bag and tube, pipe the butter in the form of a rose in the center of each anchovy.

Antipasto

Drain antipasto from the oil in which it comes and cut it in fine pieces. Season with salt, pepper and paprika and mound in one section of the compartment dish; or arrange the different relishes in a dish and place around them thin slices of tomato to form a border.

Stuffed Beets I

Select small beets and boil until tender. Cool them and peel with a fluted knife. Remove enough from the center of each to form a case. Marinate the cases for several hours in sweet pickled vinegar, drain and fill with a mixture of chopped, hard-boiled egg yolk, sardines (or anchovies), capers and gherkins; or use small pieces from a jar of antipasto.

Stuffed Beets II

Select small beets and cook until tender or use small whole canned beets. Remove enough from the center of each beet to leave a case. Marinate the cases in sweet, pickled vinegar, drain and fill with a mixture made as follows: press the yolks of hard-boiled eggs through a sieve and season with Tabasco, salt, curry powder and mayonnaise and then add chopped cress and finely chopped celery.

Cabbage Relish

Chop separately and mix: one cup of cabbage, one tablespoon of chives, one half a pimiento and two olives. Chill well and dress with a French dressing seasoned with Escoffier's Sauce *à la Diable*. Serve from a relish dish garnished with cress, or use as a filling for Rose Apples, sometimes called Pimiento Cups.

Celery Relish I

2½ cups celery cut fine	6 tablespoons sugar
6 tablespoons green pepper	3 tablespoons cornstarch
6 tablespoons onion	1 tablespoon paprika
3 tablespoons pimiento	Scant ½ teaspoon salt
⅝ cup vinegar	Dash of pepper

2 tablespoons cold water

Heat the vinegar to the boiling point, mix dry ingredients and dissolve in cold water, and then add to the vinegar. Cook until the mixture is transparent, no longer, and pour over the cut vegetables just as soon as the sauce is cooked. Mix thoroughly and chill. This will keep several days in a cold place.

Celery Relish II

Cut celery into inch-long shreds; there should be two cups. Cook these in three cups of boiling water with one teaspoon of salt until tender but not mushy and until the water has nearly evaporated. Drain well, dress with French dressing and chill thoroughly. Serve in a relish dish with a garnish of cress tips and a border of thinly sliced radishes.

Chicken Shreds Indienne

Cut the white meat of cooked chicken into inch-long shreds and marinate in French dressing to which some liquid from a bottle of chutney has been added, enough to season and make quite hot. Drain, place in a compartment dish and sprinkle the top with a few finely cut pieces of chutney.

Chicken Shreds Mexican

Cut the white meat of cooked chicken into small dice and marinate in French dressing to which curry powder has been added, then add red and green pepper cut into dice of the same size and serve in a compartment dish.

Wilted Cucumbers

Peel a cucumber with a fluted knife, so that the slices will have scalloped edges, and slice thin. Place in a dish, sprinkle the slices with salt and pepper, and half cover them with tarragon vinegar. Place on ice for two hours, stirring occasionally. When ready to serve, drain all liquid from them and place in a compartment dish. The slices will be wilted and cling together. Garnish with tiny dice of pimiento and chopped parsley.

STUFFED EGGS

Cress Eggs

3 hard-boiled eggs
5 tablespoons finely chopped cress

¾ teaspoon curry
3 tablespoons mayonnaise
Tabasco and salt

Pimiento

Cut the eggs in halves lengthwise, remove the yolks and force through a sieve. Mix well with the cress and seasonings and fill the whites. Arrange over the top of each a trellislike garnish of finely cut strips of pimiento. Place a tip of cress at one end.

Horse-radish Eggs

3 hard-boiled eggs	Worcestershire sauce
6 tablespoons grated fresh horse-radish root	2 pickled walnuts
	Paprika
3 tablespoons mayonnaise	Parsley

Cut eggs in halves lengthwise, remove the yolks and force through a sieve. Mix with horse-radish root, mayonnaise and Worcestershire sauce to season. Refill the egg whites and garnish with dots of pickled walnuts put on in diagonal rows. Sprinkle with paprika and garnish with parsley.

Lobster Eggs

Prepare hard-boiled eggs, cut in halves lengthwise, and remove yolks. Fill the whites with chopped lobster meat moistened with Sauce Tartare and invert upon oval-shaped pieces of sautéed bread. Pipe green butter over the egg and garnish with a tip of cress.

Olive Eggs

3 hard-boiled eggs	6 slices tomato
3 tablespoons butter	6 slices of bread
6 olives	½ cup aspic
6 tablespoons whipped cream	Parsley and paprika

Cut eggs in halves lengthwise and force the yolks through a sieve. Cream the butter and mix with the yolks and then add the olives, chopped, and the whipped cream. Invert the eggs, brush the outside very lightly with flour, set them upon a rack and pour over the aspic, then sprinkle with very finely chopped parsley and paprika. Set to chill and, when ready to serve, place upon a small slice of tomato placed upon a cut of sautéed bread.

Sardine Eggs

Cut three hard-boiled eggs in halves lengthwise; remove the yolks, and force through a sieve. Then mash them with enough crushed sardines to season well, with a little lemon juice and perhaps a small amount of cream to make soft. Refill the egg whites, chill and then cut the halves in halves lengthwise, and lay fine strips of pimiento diagonally over each portion.

Savory Eggs

Cut three hard-boiled eggs in halves lengthwise; remove yolks and force through a sieve. Blend with three tablespoons of creamed butter and one and one-half tablespoons of Savory Herbs cut fine, using fresh thyme, rosemary, chives, parsley and celery leaves. Fill the whites and spread over the top of each a thin layer of mayonnaise. Decorate the surface with sections of black olives.

Smoked Salmon Eggs

3 hard-boiled eggs	½ teaspoon mustard
3 tablespoons butter	Tabasco
Cold, broiled smoked	Yellow butter
salmon	Few capers

Cut the eggs in halves lengthwise and remove yolks. Force them through a sieve and combine with creamed butter and about one-third cup of finely chopped smoked salmon. Make into a smooth paste and season with mustard and Tabasco. Fill the egg whites and place the filled side down on cuts of sautéed bread. Decorate the outside with yellow butter forced through bag and tube and a few capers on the butter.

Eggs with Mustard Sauce

Cut hard-boiled eggs in lengthwise slices, using the egg slicer. Make a sauce the consistency of mayonnaise with sharp French mustard thinned with cooking wine and worked to a perfectly smooth paste. Cover the bottom of a shallow glass dish with this sauce, lay the egg slices on it and sprinkle paprika and minced parsley over the eggs.

Lobster Slices

Slice lobster meat nicely in as uniform pieces as possible and place them the length of the serving dish, overlapping one another. Then dress them with a mustard sauce or with French mustard beaten into mayonnaise dressing. Mustard seems to be the one condiment for lobster.

Salad Relish

Cut the following ingredients into inch-long, straw-like pieces and prepare an equal amount of each: cold cooked egg, potato, beet, gherkins, sardines or herring. Mix all except the beet, which should be marinated separately, and season with salt, pepper and vinegar. At the moment of serving, add the beet and also just enough stiffly beaten cream to hold all together. Serve a teaspoonful on a small lettuce leaf.

Shrimp Relish

Prepare tiny rounds of cold boiled potato (potatoes which have been cooked in their jackets the day before using) and add an equal amount of chilled shrimp. Pour over a French or Russian dressing and serve sprinkled with chopped parsley, in a compartment dish or in tiny lettuce cups.

Sweetbread and Tomatoes

Parboil sweetbreads, adding to the water lemon juice, a slice of onion, a bit of bay leaf and salt. Chill the sweetbreads and cut them into dice, then season with mayonnaise or with Russian dressing and place a layer of the mixture in a relish dish.

Cut small fresh tomatoes into sections from stem to blossom end, remove all seeds and juicy portion, marinate them in French dressing for ten minutes and then lay them over the top of the sweetbreads.

Vanderbilt Shreds

Cut a slice from the deepest yellow part of a carrot and cut into two-inch shreds. Boil until tender in salted water. Cut a green pepper in halves lengthwise, remove seeds and let stand for five minutes in boiling water to which has been added a pinch of soda. Cut in thin shreds of the same length as the carrot, having an equal amount. Slice a peeled onion lengthwise and cut into shreds, having one half as much as of the carrot. Mix and marinate thoroughly with well-seasoned French dressing. Chill well and drain, and serve in relish dish.

VII

SPREADS FOR SELF-SERVICE

Avocado Paste
Calves' Liver and Egg
Calves' Liver and Mush-
  room
Cheese Mold
Cheese, Spiced
Chicken Livers and Bacon
Chicken Livers and Mush-
  room
Chicken Salad Paste
Fish Spread
Lobster Paste

Meat and Mustard Spread
Mushroom Paste
Peanut Butter and Celery
  Spread
Radish and Scallion Spread
Salmon Spread
Smoked Salmon Spread
Sardine Spread
Sardine Whip
Shrimp Spread I
Shrimp Spread II
Spanish Rarebit

Spiced Beef Spread

Spreads for Self-Service

These various spreads or paste-like mixtures may be served from bowls or compartment dishes at the self-service party. Most of them will also make satisfactory canapé spreads, though they are not included under canapé recipes. There are also under canapé recipes many spreads which may be used here.

Avocado Paste

Mash the pulp of a well-ripened avocado with a fork and season with French dressing made with lime or lemon juice, salt, white pepper, paprika and a dash only of olive oil.

Calves' Liver and Egg

A slice of calves' liver *or*	1 teaspoon grated onion
3 chicken livers	2 tablespoons butter
3 hard-boiled eggs	Salt and pepper to season

Simmer the liver until tender, then force it through the meat chopper together with the eggs, and mix both to a paste with butter and seasonings.

Calves' Liver and Mushroom

Sauté calves' liver and force through the meat chopper. There should be one cupful. Add to this one-half cup of mushrooms which have been finely chopped and sautéed. Then season with about three tablespoons of mayonnaise, possibly more, and salt and pepper to taste.

Cheese Mold

¼ pound cottage cheese	Salt and Tabasco to taste
½ pound cream cheese	4 tablespoons capers
4 tablespoons melted butter	Pimiento-stuffed olives

Cress

Mix the two kinds of cheese and season with butter, salt, Tabasco and capers well drained. Line a mold with the olives cut in slices and press the cheese into the mold. Set it in the refrigerator to harden and unmold on a serving dish, garnishing with tips of cress.

Spiced Cheese

2 tablespoons butter	2 tablespoons cream
½ pound newly cut dairy cheese	¼ cup sherry
	1 teaspoon mustard

Salt and Tabasco to taste

Cream the butter and add to the cheese which has been forced through the meat chopper or a sieve. Moisten to a smooth paste with cream and sherry and add the dry seasonings which have been mixed together. This mixture may be arranged upon a serving dish by forcing it through a pastry bag and tube or plainly mounding it upon the dish. Another method of serving is to chill it in the refrigerator and when hard cut it into oblong sections.

Chicken Livers and Bacon

Have an equal amount of chicken livers and of bacon; that is, for eight chicken livers take eight slices of bacon. Grill the bacon very crisp and chop it fine. Sauté chicken livers in some of the bacon fat and chop fine. Combine the two and moisten to spreading consistency with a small amount of brown sauce. Season to taste.

Chicken Livers and Mushroom

Sauté four chicken livers, then sauté a cup of finely chopped mushrooms. Crush both with a fork and rub through a sieve. Season with salt, pepper and minced chives.

Chicken Salad Paste

Force cold cooked chicken and celery through the meat chopper. Moisten slightly with a boiled dressing highly seasoned with mustard. Mayonnaise may be used, though not as satisfactory.

Fish Spread

Moisten a square of cream cheese with a little cream to spreading consistency and add a fillet of anchovy cut up very fine, or use sardine or smoked salmon. Season with quite a bit of curry powder, a few chives and chopped ripe olives.

Lobster Paste

2½ cups lobster meat	1 tablespoon mustard
½ cup malt vinegar diluted	1½ tablespoons sugar
1 egg	¾ teaspoon salt
1 tablespoon flour	1 tablespoon butter

Heat the vinegar in a double boiler. Mix the dry ingredients, add an egg unbeaten, blend well and pour the hot vinegar slowly over the mixture. Cook over hot water until well thickened, cool and use. Chop lobster meat fine and moisten with this sauce.

Meat and Mustard Spread

1 tablespoon prepared mustard
¼ cup butter
½ cup minced cooked tongue

1 cup chopped cooked liver
½ cup chopped green olives
¼ cup cress or parsley, chopped

Cream the butter and mustard, then blend in the other ingredients.

Mushroom Paste

Brush, peel and stem as many mushrooms as are required, cut them rather fine and sauté in butter. Dredge with enough flour to take up the liquid in the pan and then add enough cream to make a spreading consistency. Season highly.

Peanut Butter and Celery Spread

Cream equal parts of peanut butter and dairy butter, adding salt to season, then stir in as much finely minced celery as the mixture will take up.

Radish and Scallion Spread

Chop young scallions and radishes quite fine, using half as much scallion as radish, moisten with heavy sour cream and season with salt and pepper. Serve on pumpernickel or rye bread.

Salmon Spread

Force canned salmon, or preferably fresh salmon if available, through the meat chopper and season with horse-radish mayonnaise and capers.

Smoked Salmon Spread

Slice or chop some smoked salmon, moisten to a paste with a little cream and season highly with black pepper.

Sardine Spread

Mash sardines and add just enough creamed butter to make a paste. Season mixture very highly with Tabasco and lemon juice.

Sardine Whip

Use the boneless and skinless sardines and crush them with a fork. Take about one fourth as much butter as sardine, and cream it until it will shake from the fork; combine with the sardine, add a little mayonnaise and lemon juice and beat with a fork until fluffy.

Shrimp Spread I

Grind the shrimp very fine through the meat chopper, add creamed butter to moisten, then a little cream and seasoning of salt, paprika, mustard and Worcestershire sauce.

Shrimp Spread II

Clean one can of shrimp and force through the meat chopper, add a few chives, about two tablespoons of melted butter, then lemon juice and mayonnaise to season. The paste should be quite thick, thick enough to press into a mold. Chill and, when serving, garnish with paprika, whole shrimp and a few parsley tips.

Spanish Rarebit

1 tablespoon butter
1 teaspoon finely chopped onion
1½ tablespoons chopped green pepper
⅓ cup stewed tomato

¾ pound Young America cheese
1 egg slightly beaten
Salt and cayenne to taste
2 tablespoons beer or ginger ale

Fry the pepper and onion in butter about five minutes, using an omelet pan and stirring constantly; add tomatoes, the cheese sliced thin and the seasoning. Stir over a low flame until the cheese melts; then add the egg and lastly the beer. Stir until the egg is cooked and serve either hot or cold from a bowl. This is very nice on plain crackers and just as good cold as hot, if not better.

Spiced Beef Spread

This spread is made from an old English recipe and is especially good on plain crackers. It can be kept a few days in the refrigerator.

Remove all fat from one and one-half pounds of

the top of the round. Cut the meat in ten pieces and place in a beanpot or a casserole with a cover; sprinkle with two teaspoons of salt and let stand in the refrigerator for several hours. Add one-half cup of cold water and cook in a very moderate oven for about four hours or until the meat is tender enough to tear apart. Drain the liquid from the meat into a bowl and add one-half pound of butter. Force the meat through the meat chopper into a wooden chopping bowl and add one teaspoon of white pepper and one of ground cloves. Pound the meat with a potato masher until smooth, moistening it gradually with the gravy and butter liquid. Pack into glass jelly tumblers and, if not to be used at once, pour melted butter over the top, just enough to seal it.

VIII

FIRST-COURSE OR TABLE HORS D'OEUVRE

Antipasto

Antipasto Molds

Antipasto Rings

Artichoke and Caviar Canapés

Artichoke and Lobster Canapés

Artichoke and Tuna Fish Canapés

Beets with Anchovy Filling

Crab Flakes (hot) with Tomato Jelly

Cucumber Cups with Salmon

De Luxe Rings

Eggs Ravigote

Eggs with Lobster (hot)

Ham and Chicken Savory

Lobster with Curry and Cress

Marguery Canapés for Four

Meat Rounds in Aspic

Mousse of Chicken or Ham in Aspic

Mushroom Molds

Oysters Baked on the Shell

Oysters and Spinach Baked on the Shell

Oysters Farcie

Salmon Squares

Smoked Salmon Custard Slices

Sausage and Chestnut Crusts

Sweetbreads in Tomato Jelly Rings

Sweetbreads in Tomatoes

Antipasto

Arrange the contents of a can or a jar of antipasto on slices of tomato or of toast. If using tomato place it on lettuce or on tips of cress and decorate with butter rosettes of various colors. Or the antipasto may be drained, chopped fine and spread upon toast.

Antipasto Molds

Select small timbale molds and brush them well with olive oil. Pour in a layer of tomato jelly and when it is set place a layer of finely cut antipasto to the same depth as the jelly; then add another layer of jelly and chill well. Turn out molds and garnish with cress.

Antipasto Rings

Drain antipasto well and remove some of the oil from the pieces with a paper napkin; then cut them into smaller-sized pieces.

Select very small individual ring molds and brush them generously with olive oil. Combine the antipasto with sufficient tomato jelly to hold the pieces together and pour into the molds as the jelly begins to set. Chill well and unmold each on a small lettuce leaf.

Artichoke and Caviar Canapés

Drain a can or jar of artichoke bottoms and marinate in French dressing for an hour. Drain, spread each with cream cheese moistened with cream and made quite pink with paprika. Over the cheese spread a thin layer of seasoned caviar, and over that lay a very thin slice of lemon cut like a Greek cross and garnished with parsley. Set each artichoke on a lettuce leaf, or instead of lettuce garnish with tips of cress.

Artichoke and Lobster Canapés

6 artichoke bottoms	1 pimiento
1 cup lobster meat	3 pickled walnuts
1 head lettuce	Vinegar
French dressing	Mustard
Salt, pepper and paprika	

Chop lobster with three large, green, outside lettuce leaves until both are finely shredded. Season highly with salt, pepper, dry mustard and vinegar, and chill well. Marinate artichoke bottoms in French dressing, then drain and fill with the prepared lobster. Set each one on a small lettuce leaf, sprinkle the tops with paprika and arrange in the center of each a pinwheel of small crescent-shaped pieces of pickled walnut with a spot of pimiento in the center.

Artichoke and Tuna Fish Canapés

Marinate artichoke bottoms in French dressing and place on them round sections of tuna fish. On the fish arrange the small artichokes which come in oil. Garnish with lemon and parsley.

Beets with Anchovy Filling

Select very small beets and cook until tender or use the small canned beets. Cut a slice off the top of each and reserve for a lid. Scoop out the inside of the beets until only a case is left. Fill the cases with the following mixture and serve each beet on a lettuce leaf or on a cut of toast spread lightly with anchovy paste.

To prepare the mixture, force three cold hard-boiled eggs through the potato ricer. Add one-fourth cup of cream which has been whipped, one-fourth tube of anchovy paste, and mix all together with a little mayonnaise.

Hot Crab Flakes with Cold Tomato Jelly

Make a highly spiced and seasoned tomato jelly and pour into small timbale molds. Chill well. When ready to serve, turn out on individual plates, decorate each mold with a sprig of cress, and at base, surrounding mold, place a circle of hot crab flakes, prepared as follows: —

Pick over, carefully, fresh crab flakes, and toss them in butter until well heated. Do not stir enough to break the flakes. Season with salt, pepper, Tabasco and sherry.

Cucumber Cups with Salmon

Peel a thick cucumber with a fluted knife and cut across into pieces one and one-fourth inches deep. Remove centers, leaving enough cucumber to form a thin case. Marinate these cases in French dressing, and prepare a salmon filling as follows: break cold, broiled, smoked salmon into small pieces, mix with enough Sauce Tartare to moisten, pack into the cups,

— rounding them a bit over the top, — cover with grated fresh horse-radish root and put a border of chopped green pepper around the edge.

De Luxe Rings

Place thin, circular slices of chicken or tongue on small plates and turn out on each slice a small ring mold of tomato jelly. Fill the center space with horse-radish cream (whipped cream seasoned with grated, fresh horse-radish root) and sprinkle with paprika. Place three crescent-shaped sections of ripe olives between cream and tomato jelly with black, curved side up. Garnish with tips of cress.

Eggs Ravigote

Cut hard-boiled eggs in neat slices with an egg slicer, dip the slices in Ravigote Sauce, place on lettuce and garnish with strips of pimiento and sliced, stuffed ripe olives. The sauce is a stiff mayonnaise with capers, chopped parsley, pickle and onion added. It should be thick and slightly green.

Eggs with Lobster (Hot)

Cut hard-boiled eggs in halves lengthwise, remove the yolks and fill with stuffing made as follows: put into a saucepan one-half tablespoon each of cider vinegar, tarragon vinegar, and Worcestershire sauce. Reduce to one half the quantity and add one-half cup of chopped lobster meat measured lightly. To this add one-fourth cup of white sauce, one tablespoon of butter, one teaspoon of chopped parsley and a few chopped chives. Have ready oval-shaped pieces of sautéed bread, invert the stuffed egg on the toast, shake paprika over the top and garnish with two tips of cress or parsley and a tip of a lobster claw. This amount will fill ten egg halves.

Ham and Chicken Savory

Cut rounds two inches in diameter from one-eighth-inch slices of cold boiled ham. Spread these rounds with a chicken paste made of white meat forced through a sieve and seasoned with mayonnaise and chopped chives. Over the chicken lay a slice of tomato jelly or tomato aspic of the same size. Brush the sides with aspic and chill. Serve each form on a lettuce leaf or garnish with cress tips.

Lobster with Curry and Cress

Cut lettuce leaves with a round cutter and place on each round a teaspoon of minced lobster seasoned with curry and French dressing. Mask the mound entirely with cress leaves.

Canapé Marguery for Four

Have the following ingredients chopped together and at hand, also have a Russian dressing ready in a bowl.

1 hard-boiled egg	2 peeled tomatoes
Tuna fish to equal the	6 fillets of anchovy
amount of egg	½ a green pepper

Sauté four slices of bread in a chafing dish until well crisped or have them brought in from the kitchen on a heated platter. Then divide the mixture to cover the four slices of toast and finish with a spoonful of Russian dressing and several drops of Worcestershire sauce over each serving.

Meat Rounds in Aspic

Cut smoked tongue in rounds one-fourth inch thick. Spread them with chicken paste made of puréed white meat of chicken combined with mayonnaise and a little chutney. Set the rounds on a rack and pour over them a partially chilled tomato aspic or a jellied Consommé Madrilène. Chill and garnish with cress tips.

Mousse of Chicken or Ham in Aspic

Make a mousse of either chicken or ham (see your cookbook) and when cold cut into forms. Dip these forms into tomato jelly or tomato aspic, let harden and serve on cress.

Mushroom Molds

Chop mushrooms rather fine, sauté in as little butter as possible, and season with chopped chives and parsley, salt and white pepper. Then combine with aspic, using only enough to hold the mushrooms together, and fill very small molds.

Oysters Baked on the Shell

1 teaspoon finely chopped onion	6 oysters on the half shell
1 clove garlic	2 to 3 tablespoons finely sifted bread crumbs
2 teaspoons chives	3 slices bacon
⅓ cup sweet butter	Rock salt

Chop onion, garlic and chives very fine and pound with a wooden mallet. Then mix with the butter and rub through a fine sieve. Place the oysters on the half shell, cover them with the prepared butter, sprinkle with a few bread crumbs and then lay over each a small, thin piece of bacon. Place the filled shells on a bed of rock salt in a baking pan and put into a hot oven for about ten minutes or until the bacon is crisp. This serves only two people.

Oysters and Spinach Baked on the Shell

18 oysters on the half shell	Grated Gruyère cheese
1½ cups cooked spinach	Fine, sifted bread crumbs
¼ cup cream	Tarragon vinegar
2 tablespoons flour	Salt and pepper
	Rock salt

Prepare the spinach by cooking it with a bit of soda in the water; then chop it fine and mix with the cream and flour and season highly. Put a spoonful of this spinach mixture in the bottom of each half shell and using a spoon, sprinkle a few drops of the vinegar over each one. Lay an oyster on the spinach in each shell, cover it with a thin layer of cheese and the finest of bread crumbs and put under the broiler until the crumbs are brown. If you have fresh tarragon leaves, chop fine and sprinkle them over the tops.

Oysters Farcie

For six people chop six large oysters and put into a saucepan with one teaspoon of cracker crumbs, two tablespoons butter, one-fourth cup of heavy cream, a dash of mace and cayenne and salt if necessary. Heat thoroughly and heap on the uncooked side of small cuts of bread which have been sautéed on one side only.

Salmon Squares

Have cold boiled salmon from one and one-half to two inches in thickness cut into neat squares. Set these upon a rack and pour over a mayonnaise to which is added a little dissolved gelatin. Place a shrimp on top of each square and a very small sprig of cress or of parsley in the center of the shrimp. Chill well.

Smoked Salmon Custard Slices

Select a very small bread pan, one of those used for individual loaves of bread. Butter the pan well and cover the bottom with a layer of very thinly sliced smoked salmon. Make the salmon as thin as possible by pressing the slice with a knife. Then place a layer of thinly sliced boiled potato (freshly boiled without peeling and cooled), then again a slice of salmon and layer of potato until the pan is filled to within one-half inch of the top. Each layer of salmon should be sprinkled with freshly ground pepper.

Prepare an unseasoned egg custard in the proportion of one-half cup of milk to one egg and add to the contents of the pan; make one or two incisions in the layers so that the custard can seep through the mixture. Place the pan in a larger pan of hot water and bake at a low temperature. When the custard is set, cool and slice, using a very sharp knife. Serve a slice individually with a tip of cress.

Sausage and Chestnut Crusts

Prepare toast shapes and cover with thin slices of cooked sausage, then a spoonful of cooked chestnuts combined with a brown sauce.

Sweetbreads in Tomato Jelly Rings

Mold highly seasoned tomato jelly in small, individual ring molds and invert on small plates. Cut tiny cubes from sweetbreads which have been parboiled with a bit of bay leaf, a slice of onion and two tablespoons of lemon juice in the water. Marinate these cubes for a few hours in a French dressing made of tarragon vinegar. When ready to serve, drain the cubes from the dressing and fill the rings. Sprinkle finely chopped parsley over the sweetbreads and garnish with tips of cress.

Sweetbreads in Tomatoes

Chop a parboiled sweetbread very fine and season with mayonnaise. Remove centers from small tomatoes, sprinkle the inside of the cases with salt and pepper, invert for a half hour and then fill them with the prepared sweetbread; or the mixture may be heaped on a slice of tomato.

IX

MISCELLANEOUS RECIPES

Asparagus Rolls (hot)
Caviar Bouchées
Caviar Pastry Stars
Cheese Cups
Cheese Fancies
Cheese Filling
Cheese Pastries
Chicken and Chutney
  Turnovers or Rissoles
  (hot)
Curried Crab Meat Bou-
  chées (hot)
Finnan Haddie Bouchées
  (hot)
Ham Bouchées (hot)
Liver, Egg and Bacon
  Turnovers
Meat Turnovers
Mushroom Bouchées
  (hot)

Parmesan Cheese Sticks
Parsley Crescents
Parsley Crusts
Sweetbread and Mush-
  room Bouchées (hot)
Tomato Aspic
Tomato Jelly
Dressings
  French Dressing I
  French Dressing II
  Curry French Dress-
    ing
  Epicurean French Dress-
    ing
  Mayonnaise
  Russian Mayonnaise
  Mustard Dressing
    (cooked)
  Roquefort Dressing
  Vinaigrette Sauce

Asparagus Rolls (Hot)

Spread squares of thinly sliced dark bread with savory or anchovy butter, wrap it around a cooked asparagus tip which has been well drained, and toast. The squares may be made more pliable to roll without cracking if first rolled with a rolling-pin.

Caviar Bouchées

Make a choux paste mixture for which consult your cookbook. Shape small rounds, using pastry bag and tube; when baked they should be about the size of a fifty-cent piece. Cool and fill with caviar well seasoned and chilled.

Caviar Pastry Stars

Cut thinly rolled puff paste in small star shapes and bake. When cooled, split and fill with seasoned caviar. Pipe green savory butter in a design over the top.

Cheese Cups

Slice bread one-half inch thick and cut into squares. Scoop out centers, leaving tiny cases. Toss these in hot butter until quite brown. Fill each with grated factory cheese seasoned with cayenne and put into oven to melt the cheese and further brown the bread. They may be varied by laying a tiny square of bacon over the cheese before baking.

Cheese Fancies

½ cup pastry flour
⅛ teaspoon salt
⅛ teaspoon paprika
½ cup grated
  cheese

1½ tablespoons olive oil
About 4 tablespoons of cold
  water
2 tablespoons grated
  cheese for tops

Mix flour, seasonings and cheese and, using a knife, cut in the oil, then mix to a stiff paste with cold water. Chill and roll very, very thin. Stamp out rounds with a scalloped cutter about two inches in diameter, sprinkle with more grated cheese and bake in a rather moderate oven. Prick with a fork before baking. When they are removed from oven, sprinkle with paprika. They are ruined if the heat is too strong.

Cheese Filling

1½ tablespoons butter
2 tablespoons flour
⅔ cup milk
1 egg yolk

½ cup mild cheese
¼ cup grated Gruyère
  cheese
Salt, pepper and cayenne

Possibly a little cream

Melt butter, add flour and, when smooth, the milk and then the egg yolk unbeaten. Add the cheese, keep over the fire until the cheese is melted, then season to taste. Some kinds of cheese thicken more than others so that it may be necessary to add a little cream to make a creamy consistency.

Cheese Pastries

Make puff paste; roll one fourth of an inch thick and cut in oval shapes rather long and narrow. Bake in a hot oven about 400° F. Cool, split and fill with the preceding cheese mixture, which should be creamy and soft. Sprinkle the tops with paprika. These are especially liked for teas.

Chicken and Chutney Turnovers or Rissoles (Hot)

Combine finely chopped chicken with chopped chutney to moisten and season highly with curry. It may be necessary to add a little heavy cream or chicken stock to make the mixture sufficiently moist. Use as a filling for small turnovers. Bake them or fry them in deep fat as rissoles.

Curried Crab Meat Bouchées (Hot)

Moisten one cup of crab meat with lemon juice, a little tarragon vinegar, and season to taste with salt, cayenne, mustard and a dash of nutmeg. Then add one-fourth cup of dried bread crumbs which have been fried in butter. Make small bread cases, brush over with butter and bake until brown. Put a spoonful of the crab mixture in the center hollow, mask it with a thick curry sauce, sprinkle over that buttered crumbs and bake until the crumbs are brown.

Finnan Haddie Bouchées (Hot)

2 cups flaked cooked finnan
    haddie
1 slice onion finely chopped
1 tablespoon finely chopped
    green pepper
1 tablespoon finely chopped
    pimiento

¼ cup butter
4 tablespoons flour
¾ cup cream
¾ cup milk
Salt and cayenne to season

Sauté onion and peppers in butter for five minutes, add flour and pour on slowly, stirring constantly, the milk and cream. Bring to the boiling point and add finnan haddie. Season and use to fill small pastry cases.

Ham Bouchées (Hot)

Chop lean, cooked ham and measure six tablespoonfuls. Put the ham into a saucepan with two eggs slightly beaten, one medium-sized peeled tomato and one tablespoon of heavy cream. Stir over the fire until thickened and fill very small patty cases with the mixture. Place a small sautéed mushroom on top. This amount fills seven cases.

Liver, Egg and Bacon Turnovers

½ cup minced, cooked liver
1 cup minced, broiled bacon
½ hard-boiled egg chopped

1 tablespoon parsley
⅛ teaspoon curry
Salt and pepper

Combine ingredients and make into small pastry turnovers.

Meat Turnovers

1 cup of chopped, cooked meat	2 tablespoons flour
	½ cup meat stock
2 tablespoons butter	Salt and pepper
Thyme and onion juice	

Make a sauce of butter, flour and stock, and season highly, using fresh thyme if available; if not, the dried will do. Add the meat forced through the meat chopper.

Make plain paste, and cut in rounds, making a few cuts in the upper half. Place on the rounds a spoonful of the meat filling, wet the edges, press them together and bake in a quick oven.

Mushroom Bouchées (Hot)

Chop one shallot fine, or use one-half teaspoon of finely chopped onion and sauté in two tablespoons of butter. When brown, add one-fourth pound of mushrooms chopped fine. Sauté till done, then add three hard-boiled eggs chopped fine and also one tablespoon of chopped parsley. Season with salt, cayenne and a small amount of Vegex. Fill puff-paste bouchées with this mixture and place a small sautéed mushroom on top of each.

Parmesan Cheese Sticks

Use bread twenty-four hours old, remove crusts and slice as thin as possible without breaking the slices. Cut slices into strips about one and one-fourth inches wide and three inches long. Have ready a small shallow pan of melted butter, into which dip the sticks. Pick them up with the point of a French knife, hold them until the butter ceases to drip, then drop them into a dish of grated Parmesan cheese. It is better to grate the cheese oneself than to use bottled grated cheese. Using the fingers, coat them entirely with the cheese and place on a baking sheet. Run them under a gas flame and brown well, turn with a spatula, and brown under side. Drain on soft, clean paper. These can be prepared two or three hours in advance and kept in a warm place.

Parsley Crescents

Cut stale bread in one-fourth-inch slices and stamp out forms with a small crescent cutter. Toast slightly, brush upper side with melted butter and then dip this side in parsley which has been chopped with a knife. Be careful that parsley is not wet when chopped. Return under the flame and remove as soon as the parsley takes on a vivid green. A moment too long will make it brown and undesirable. For a Christmas party the bread may be cut in small star shapes.

Parsley Crusts

Slice crisp French rolls lengthwise through the center and spread the two sections with parsley butter made in the proportion of one half as much finely chopped parsley as butter. After spreading the cut surface of the rolls slice vertically in half-inch widths, not cutting through the bottom crust. Place on a baking sheet in a 375° F. oven to become hot and crusty. Arrange on serving dish; the slices will break apart easily.

Sweetbread and Mushroom Bouchées (Hot)

Parboil sweetbreads with a slice of onion and a bit of bay leaf in the water; chill and cut into very small dice.

Brush, peel and stem mushrooms; cut small and sauté in butter. Sauté the sweetbreads in butter until they are slightly brown, combine them with the mushrooms and add to the following sauce, using only enough of the sauce to hold the mixture together. When mushrooms are out of season, a few chopped pimientos may be used.

Sauce. Melt two tablespoons of butter, add three tablespoons of flour, one-half cup each of milk and cream and about one-fourth cup of sherry. Add salt and paprika to taste and fill pastry bouchées.

Tomato Aspic

Put one quart of canned tomatoes into a saucepan with the following: —

1 cup of celery cut small	3 cloves
⅓ cup carrot	1 teaspoon peppercorns
2 tablespoons sliced onion	Small piece of mace
Sprig of parsley	1 teaspoon salt
	1 green pepper cut small
Dash of cayenne	

Cook twenty or thirty minutes, strain and cool. Add gelatin which has been softened in cold water, using the proportion of one tablespoon to one cup of tomato, and clear.

Tomato Jelly

1 pint canned tomato	6 cloves
3 slices onion	Small piece of mace
4 stalks celery cut small	Bit of bay leaf
2 slices carrot	1 tablespoon sugar
Sprig of parsley	Salt and Tabasco to taste
1½ teaspoons peppercorns	Gelatin

Cook the tomatoes with all seasonings except the Tabasco for twenty minutes and strain. Add gelatin softened in cold water, using the proportion of three-fourths tablespoon to one cup of liquid. Then add Tabasco. Stir until dissolved and set to chill.

DRESSINGS

French Dressing I

¼ teaspoon mustard	¼ teaspoon salt
1 teaspoon powdered sugar	Dash of cayenne
⅛ teaspoon black pepper	2 tablespoons vinegar
4 tablespoons olive oil	

Put dry ingredients into a small bowl set in cracked ice and let all become perfectly cold. Then add the chilled vinegar and, beating all the time with an egg beater, slowly add the oil. The result will be a very thick, smooth dressing.

French Dressing II

Mix thoroughly in a bowl two teaspoons of sugar and one-fourth teaspoon each of mustard, salt and paprika; add one tablespoon each of oil and of vinegar and beat well with the egg beater; then add two more tablespoons of oil, again beat well, and add one more tablespoon of vinegar and lastly three tablespoons of oil. Beat well and the result will be a very heavy French dressing which will keep in the refrigerator some time without separating.

Curry French Dressing

¼ teaspoon salt	1 tablespoon vinegar
1 teaspoon curry powder	¼ cup olive oil

The chef who served this dressing put all the ingredients into a saucepan, brought them to the boiling point, then set the pan in iced water and beat with an egg beater until dressing was cold. One may simply add curry powder to the rule for French dressing if wished.

Epicurean French Dressing

1 teaspoon salt	1 tablespoon finely chopped
½ teaspoon powdered sugar	onion
5 tablespoons vinegar	2 tablespoons finely
½ cup olive oil	chopped parsley

Red Pepper Sauce

Mix dressing well and set on ice for two hours before serving. Use about nine inch-long peppers from the sauce. These peppers give a fine flavor but should be removed from the dressing before serving as they are extremely hot.

Mayonnaise

This recipe is given instead of the real egg and oil mayonnaise for the reason that it stands up better, is firmer and can be used with less fear of separation.

2 tablespoons sugar	1 unbeaten egg
1 tablespoon mustard	¼ cup cornstarch
1 tablespoon salt	¼ cup cold water
Dash of cayenne	1 cup boiling water
1 cup olive oil	2 tablespoons vinegar

3 tablespoons lemon juice

Put dry seasonings into a quart bowl and mix. Then without stirring add the oil and the egg. Let these stand while preparing the cornstarch mixture. Into a small saucepan put the cornstarch and make smooth with the cold water. Add the boiling water and stir rapidly over the flame until the mixture becomes transparent, then add to the first mixture and beat rapidly with an egg beater. When the mixture thickens and becomes smooth, beat in the acids and chill.

Russian Mayonnaise

¾ cup mayonnaise	2 tablespoons finely cut
Juice from a fresh tomato	pimiento
1 tablespoon tarragon vine-	1 teaspoon Escoffier Sauce
gar	(*à la Diable*)

1 teaspoon cut chives

Mix the mayonnaise with the strained juice from a fresh tomato, perhaps two if the tomato is small, and the vinegar; then add remaining ingredients. Many use chili sauce instead of tomato juice, but the latter will be found to be a great improvement, resulting in a dressing not so heavy in flavor.

Mustard Dressing (Cooked)

½ cup vinegar	2 teaspoons mustard
3 tablespoons butter	½ teaspoon salt
3 teaspoons flour	Dash of cayenne
2 teaspoons sugar	2 egg yolks

Scald the vinegar diluted one half if very strong and melt the butter in the vinegar. Mix flour and sugar with seasonings and add to the egg yolks slightly beaten. Pour the hot vinegar over this, return to the double boiler and cook until thickened, stirring constantly. Strain and cool.

Roquefort Dressing

Mash four ounces of Roquefort cheese until smooth, using a wooden spoon; add a dash each of salt, cayenne and paprika. To this mixture add slowly two tablespoons of vinegar, six tablespoons of olive oil and, the last thing, two tablespoons of heavy, sweet cream.

Vinaigrette Sauce

1 teaspoon salt	6 tablespoons olive oil
⅛ teaspoon paprika	1 tablespoon chopped chives
Dash of Tabasco	1 teaspoon chopped parsley
2 tablespoons malt vinegar	1 teaspoon chopped capers

Mix the first four ingredients, add the oil slowly, beating with the egg beater, and when quite thick add the remaining ingredients.

X

VARIED COMBINATIONS FOR SERVING HORS D'OEUVRE

CENTERPIECES FOR PLATTERS OF HORS D'OEUVRE

I. Scrape radishes so that they are white with tinges of red and be sure to leave a tip of green leaf at the base; then cut them into fancy shapes and let stand in ice water to open. Make a center mound of these radishes with some curled celery; the white center is quite effective and should be surrounded with canapés which are colorful.

II. Arrange a mound of sardines to run up to a point; this should give height and also furnish an attractive silvery tone for a center around which group selected hors d'oeuvre.

III. Cut three large tomatoes into poinsettia shape and include a few small tomatoes for buds, barely opening the petals of the small ones. Raise these by placing them on a thick bed of parsley, cress or, what is very effective, finely shredded light green cabbage. Select canapés to fit the color scheme and arrange them around this center.

IV. Place a large bunch of parsley in the center of the serving dish. Cut the stems of the outer sprays short or entirely off in order to form a round bunch; then toss on carelessly small dots cut from very red pimientos; a small plain icing tube will cut the right size. This arrangement is especially attractive for the Christmas season. The canapés should be chosen to harmonize.

V. Form a line of parsley sprays through the center of a platter and sprinkle with red dots of pimiento which will resemble berries. Place canapés on each side of the platter.

VI. Set a perfect head of cauliflower into a frying basket and cook in strongly salted water so carefully that it may be lifted out whole. In order to keep the shape it should not be overcooked. Chill it and decorate with a border of finely minced parsley at the base and above that a border of paprika.

VII. Shape hard-boiled eggs into pond lilies with mashed yolk centers and arrange on dark green lettuce leaves either shredded or whole. Then place around these a border of decorative canapés.

VIII. Select a glass or a silver bowl and fill it with iced vegetables, an assortment of which may be chosen from the following: curled celery, stick-like cuts of Chinese cabbage, sections of crisp fennel, scallions, cucumbers cut in lengthwise sections, French endive, young new carrots sliced lengthwise very thin and dropped into ice water until they curl, radishes scraped and unscraped, and tips of cress.

Set the bowl in the center of a large flat serving dish and fill in the space around the base of the bowl with sprigs of parsley or of cress, taking care that no stems show. A few light tips of celery look well with the dark green and at Christmas time clusters of cranberries may be used among the sprays. Arrange canapés around the edge, or tiny, highly seasoned meat turn-overs, or filled pastry cases.

CENTERPIECES FOR PIERCED SAVORIES

I. A perfect eggplant, fresh, plump and glossy, with parsley or cress tucked around its base, is an effective background for pierced savories.

II. A honeydew melon gives a good background, both in color and in size, especially for colorful savories; or one may use halves of melon filled with radish roses, curled celery and olives, and insert pierced savories around the edge.

III. A fresh cabbage, either purple, green or white, may be scooped out and filled with cole slaw in addition to being used for skewered savories.

IV. A cabbage may be hollowed to form a case and filled with Russian dressing, and the pierced savories consist of shrimp and flowerets of cold cooked cauliflower.

V. Select a long, slim, fresh-looking cucumber. Rub it lightly with olive oil to ensure a shiny surface and set it in the center of the serving dish on a bed of some salad green. (Chicory is especially good.) This makes an admirable center for speared savories.

VI. Remove the top of a pineapple cheese, making cuts in such a way that when the top is removed the cheese will be in points. A large green or black glass plate is effective for this centerpiece. Place a cheese knife on top of the cheese and impale the pierced savories which you select into the sides of the cheese. Tuck celery tips with no stems showing around the base and use popular canapés to finish the edge of the plate.

VII. Cut off the top of an Edam cheese, scoop out the center, mash it to a paste, seasoning well with mustard and Worcestershire sauce, and refill the shell. The pierced savories may then be stuck into the sides at intervals, with canapés to border it.

VIII. Remove crusts from a loaf of bread, butter it all over and brown in the oven; then sprinkle it with paprika and finely minced parsley. This makes a good foundation for hot savories on skewers.

IX. A large round loaf of Italian bread is also good
for hot relishes such as fried oysters, tiny fish
balls, small sausages, chicken livers in bacon, etc.
Stuffed celery, celery trees, cuts of Chinese cabbage and radish roses are appetizing accompaniments to the hot hors d'oeuvre.

X. A terraced loaf of bread prepared by the following directions will prove an unusual base for
pierced savories. Remove the crust from the top,
sides and ends of a large sandwich loaf. At each
end of the loaf make a horizontal cut one and
one-half inches from the bottom and three inches
toward the center of the loaf. Cut down from
the top and remove this three-inch section; this
is the first step of the terrace.

For the second step, make a cut one and one-half
inches up on the solid loaf and three inches
toward the center, then cut down from the top
to meet it and remove the second section. Brush
the bread generously with melted butter and
brown well in the oven, turning frequently to
brown evenly. This terrace may be used for
hot or for cold skewered savories. Arrange a
border of canapés and use cress to separate them
from the centerpiece.

XI. Select a smooth, shapely grapefruit and remove
a thin slice from the bottom so that it will set
firmly on the dish. Cut the center from a seven-
or eight-inch lace-paper doily and slip the re-

maining circle over the grapefruit to about the center, where it can be held in place by inserting toothpicks in the grapefruit directly under it. Then use the upper half for skewered savories and place canapés on the dish as a border.

XII. One may purchase perforated forms of wood, china and other materials in which the skewered hors d'oeuvre may be inserted.

PLATTER ARRANGEMENTS OF HORS D'OEUVRE

I. Whip up cream cheese with a little melted butter, salt and white pepper, and divide into four portions. Fold chopped chutney to taste into one portion, mix chopped chives and pimiento into the second portion, add coarsely chopped watermelon pickle to another, and into the last fold finely chopped celery or chopped fresh herbs. Make mounds of the four different flavors of cheese on a serving dish and arrange cress tips to separate them.

II. Arrange sprays of parsley with no stems showing through the length and center of a tray or platter, and sprinkle the parsley with dots of bright red pimiento. On one side arrange a long mound of cottage cheese which has been seasoned with chopped olives, chopped chives and cream, and on the other side use cream cheese seasoned with melted butter, Worcestershire sauce and chopped fresh herbs.

III. Combine cream cheese with the following seasonings: Worcestershire sauce, a dash of scraped onion, salt, paprika, pepper and a little mayonnaise. Make a rough mound of this mixture in the center of a low dish and surround it with crisp potato chips which the guests may use as edible scoops. Sautéed chopped mushrooms combined with cream cheese, salt and pepper make a delicious blend.

IV. Make a ring mold of finely chopped cooked beets mixed with high seasonings and aspic, and chill. Turn out and heap in the center flowerets of marinated cooked cauliflower, tiny white glazed onions, the smallest hothouse tomatoes available (and in season small yellow ones) and stuffed olives, both ripe and green. The effect is quite striking with a border of cress and simple canapés.

V. Fill with shaved ice a large pyrex shallow dish, either square or oblong in shape. Set three bowls in the ice, one containing fresh caviar, another a cocktail sauce and the third holding mayonnaise. Around the bowls on nests of lettuce have small servings of shrimp, crab meat, lobster, etc. mixed lightly with French dressing. Place ripe

olives and slices of lemon around the edge of
the dish. The lettuce should be crisp and every-
thing as cold as possible.

Guests serve themselves, using small plates which
may be used upon the table or passed. Plain
sandwiches of both dark and white bread made
with savory butter should be served or, if preferred, small unbuttered finger rolls.

VI. A sea-food platter for a buffet spread makes an
appealing set-up. Arrange in the center of a
large platter the tail shells of as many small lob-
sters as required, filled with lobster meat cut in
small pieces and seasoned highly. A curry
French dressing is particularly good.

Bordering the lobster alternate small tomatoes
filled with seasoned crab meat (a spot of caviar
may or may not be used for garnish) and small
green peppers, or large ones cut in halves, filled
with shrimp salad, and for the border alternate
boneless sardines on toast and small squares of
cold boiled salmon masked with mayonnaise
and sprinkled with capers. A little gelatin may
be added to the mayonnaise for firmness.

VII. A pleasing caviar service is to place a silver bowl
containing cracked ice in the center of a silver
platter and imbed in the ice a glass bowl filled
with caviar. Around the caviar arrange small

dishes containing sifted egg yolk, chopped white of egg, chopped onion and sections of lemon. Also provide finger-shaped pieces of toast the corners of which may be clipped or not.

TRAY COMBINATIONS FOR ASSORTED CANAPÉS

Cold

I. Arrange a bunch of parsley in the center of a chop plate and sprinkle over it a few dots of pimiento. Then place around this center alternately

> Caviar Canapés III (p. 29)
> Pimiento Stars (p. 57)
> Sardine Canapés III (p. 36)

II. Set up a small oval tray with

> Celery Trees (p. 76) standing lengthwise through the center and around them alternate Tomato Canapés (p. 57) and Chicken Liver Canapés I (p. 47)

III. Arrange a row of

> Lobster Canapés I (p. 34) through the center of a tray and on each side alternate Vegetable Canapés (p. 58) and Gruyère Croutons (p. 53)

Place at each end a garnish of cress or parsley with a cut radish tucked into the green for color.

IV. Heap a mound of
Cheese Truffles (p. 69) in the center of a
round serving dish and surround with
Ham and Ripe Olive Canapés (p. 45) and
Pâté de Foie Gras Canapés, any one given
(pp. 48, 49)

V. Heap a mound of
East Indian Cheese Balls (p. 68) in the center
of a round dish and surround with
Chicken Canapés (p. 43) and
Sardine Ovals (p. 37)

VI. Arrange six kinds of canapés across the width
of a large tray or platter and separate the rows
with slender lines of cress tips. This is rather
more elaborate than the preceding combinations
yet the idea may be carried out with canapés
which involve less work.
Lobster Medallions (p. 35)
Spanish Canapés (p. 54)
Deviled Ham Canapés (p. 45)
Fish Mousse Croutons (p. 32)
Fan Canapés (p. 56)
Cheese and Olive Canapés (p. 52)

Hot

I. Heap Asparagus Rolls (p. 109) lengthwise
through the center of an oblong tray and on
each side place alternately

Mushroom Fingers (p. 56) and
Shrimp Canapés Indienne (p. 38)

II. Through the center of a tray place a row of
Parsley Crusts (p. 114) and border them with
Calves' Liver Squares (p. 65)
Smoked Salmon Balls (p. 63) and
Hot Cheese Balls (p. 68), all on skewers

III. In the center of a shallow dish, plate or platter,
place two rows of
Sweetbread and Mushroom Bouchées (p. 115),
then border them with
Sardine Canapés II (p. 36) and
Cheese and Olive Canapés I (p. 51)

IV. Arrange the following hors d'oeuvre across the
width of a platter or a long tray
Curried Crab Meat Bouchées (p. 111), three
rows, through the center
Cheese and Almond Canapés (p. 50) on one
side of center
Ham and Mushroom Crusts (p. 44) on opposite side

V. In the center of a chop plate, heap a mound of
Deviled Shrimp (p. 63) and alternate a bor-
der of
Bacon and Cheese Canapés (p. 41) and
Curried Lobster Canapés (p. 34) or
Mushroom Fingers (p. 56)

VI. In the center of a chop plate or a platter arrange
a mound of
Liver, Egg and Bacon Turnovers (p. 112)
and place around them
Sardine Canapés II (p. 36) and
Chicken and Ham Canapés (p. 44) or
Sweetbread Canapés (p. 49)

INDEX

A

ANCHOVIES, 8
with Pimiento Butter, 80
Anchovy and Caviar Canapés,
    30
    Balls, 75
    Butter, 22
    Canapés I, 28
    Canapés II, 28
    Filling for Beets, 99
Almond and Cheese Canapés,
    50
Antipasto, 8, 98
    Molds, 98
    Rings, 98
Artichoke and Caviar Cana-
pés, 98
    and Lobster Canapés, 99
    and Tuna Fish Canapés,
    99
Artichokes and Bacon, 64
Asparagus Rolls, 109
Aspic, Meat Rounds in, 103
    Mousse of Chicken in, 103
    Tomato, 115
Avocado Cubes, 71
    Paste, 90

B

BACON AND ARTICHOKES, 64
    and Cheese Canapés, 41
    and Cheese Croquettes, 68

and Chicken Liver
    Spread, 91
and Chicken Livers, 64
and Peanut Butter Cana-
    pés, 42
and Prunes Baked, 64
and Scallops, 62
and Tomato Canapés I,
    42, II, 43
and Watermelon Pickle,
    65
Bacon Crisps with Peanut
    Butter, 65
Balls, Anchovy, 75
    Cheese, Cream, 68
    Cheese, East Indian, 68
    Cheese Footballs, 69
    Cheese, Gruyère, 69
    Cheese (hot), 75
    Cheese Snacks, 69
    Cheese Truffles, 69
    Chipped Beef, 66
    Fish, 61
    Fish, Surprise (Bacon),
        61
    (Piccalilli), 61
    Ham, 66
    Nut, 70
    Smoked Salmon, 63
Beef, Chipped, Balls, 66
    Spiced, Spread, 95
Beets, Stuffed, I, 81, II, 81
    with Anchovy Filling,
        99

Bouchées, Caviar, 109
    Crab Meat, Curried, 111
    Finnan Haddie, 112
    Ham, 112
    Mushroom, 113
    Sweetbread and Mush-
      room, 115
Broiled Sardines, 38
Butters, Flavored, 21
    Anchovy, 22
    Cheese, 22
    Chive, 22
    Cress, 22
    Curry, 23
    Green Pepper, 23
      Savory, 23
    Horse-radish, 24
    Mustard, 24
    Parsley, 24
    Pimiento, 24
    Red, 25
    Savory, I, 25, II, 25
    Tomato Catsup, 26
    Vegex or Maggi, 26
    Yellow, 26

C

CABBAGE RELISH, 81
Calves' Liver and Egg Spread,
    90
    and Mushroom Spread,
    90
    Bacon and Egg Turn-
      overs, 112
    Canapés, 46
    Squares, 65
Canapés, Almond and Cheese,
    50
    Anchovy I, 28, II, 28
    and Caviar, 30

Artichoke and Caviar, 98
    and Lobster, 98
    and Tuna Fish, 99
Bacon and Cheese, 41
    and Peanut Butter, 42
    and Tomato I, 42, II, 43
Caviar I, 28, II, 29, III, 29,
    IV, 29
    and Anchovy, 30
    and Tomato, 31
    Latticed, 31
    (Russell), 29
    (Russian), 30
Cheese and Chive, 51
    and Nut, 51
    and Olive I, 51, II, 52
    and Pimiento, 52
    Daisies, 52
Chicken, 43
    and Ham, 44
    and Liver I, 47, II, 47,
    III, 47
    Curried, 43
    Salad, 44
Crab Meat, 32
Fan, 56
Finnan Haddie, 32
Fish Mousse, 32
Ham and Chicken, 44
    and Mushroom Crusts,
    44
    and Mustard, 45
    and Ripe Olive, 45
    Chicken Liver and
    Mushroom, 45
    Deviled, 45
    Medallions, 46
    Mushroom and Cream
    Cheese, 46
Herring I, 33, II, 33
Liver, Calves', 46

Chicken I, 47, II, 47,
  III, 47
  or Calves', 47
Lobster, I, 34, II, 34
  Curried, 34
  Medallions, 35
  Pickled, 35
Lucerne, 53
Marguery, 102
Meat Paste, 48
Mushroom Fingers, 56
Olive and Cheese I, 51,
  II, 52
  and Sardine, 37
Pâté de Foie Gras I, 48,
  II, 48, III, 49, IV, 49
Peanut Butter and Bacon,
  42
Pimiento and Cheese, 52
  Stars, 57
Radish, 57
Sardine I, 36, II, 36, III,
  36, IV, 36, V, 37, VI,
  37
  and Olive, 37
  Ovals, 37
Shrimp, 38
  and Cress, 39
  Indienne, 38
Smoked Salmon and
  Cream Cheese, 40
  Caviar and Anchovy,
  40
  Danish, 39
Spanish, 54
Sweetbread, 49
Tomato, 57
Valentine, 58
Vegetable, 58
Volendam I, 55, II, 55
Capers, 9

Cauliflower and Shrimp, 71
  Sprigs, 72
Caviar, 9
  and Anchovy Canapés, 30
  and Artichoke Canapés,
  98
  and Cress Sandwiches, 30
  and Tomato Canapés, 31
  Bits, 31
  Blackberries, 60
  Bouchées, 109
  Canapés I, 28–29, II, 29,
  III, 29, IV, 29
  Latticed, 31
  (Russell), 29
  (Russian), 30
  Smoked Salmon and
  Anchovy, 40
  Fishes, 31
  Pastry Stars, 109
Celery and Peanut Butter
  Spread, 93
  Relish I, 82, II, 82
  Stalks, Stuffed, 76
  Trees, 76
Cheese Balls, Cream, 68
  East Indian, 68
  Gruyère, 69
  Footballs, 69
  (hot), 68
  Butter, 22
  Canapés with Almonds,
  50
  Croquettes with Bacon, 68
  Cups, 109
  Daisies, 52
  Fancies, 110
  Lucerne Canapés, 53
  Mold, 90
  Oysterettes, 76
  Parmesan Sticks, 113

Cheese (*continued*)
    Pastries, 111
    Roquefort Wafers, 54
    Rusks, Savory, 54
    Snacks, 69
    Spanish, 54
    Spiced, 91
    Truffles, 69
    Volendam I, 55, II, 55
    with Bacon, 41
    with Chives, 51
    with Nuts, 51
    with Olives (cold), 52
      (hot), 51
    with Pimiento, 52
Cheesehill Wafers, 53
Chestnut and Sausage Crusts, 106
Chestnuts, Glazed, 72
Chicken and Chutney Turn-overs, 111
    and Ham Canapés, 44
      Savory, 102
    Canapés, 43
    Curried Canapés, 43
    Liver and Bacon Spread, 91
      and Mushroom Spread, 92
    Mousse in Aspic, 103
    Salad Canapés, 44
      Paste or Spread, 92
    Shreds, Indienne, 82
      Mexican, 83
Chipped Beef Balls, 66
Chive and Cheese Canapés, 51
Chive Butter, 22
Chutney, 9
    and Chicken Turnovers, 111
Consommé, 10

Crab Meat Canapés, 32
    Curried, Bouchées, 111
    Flakes with Tomato Jelly, 100
Cream Cheese and Nut Balls, 70
    Canapés, 51
    and Smoked Salmon Buds, 63
    and Smoked Salmon Canapés, 40
    Balls, 68
    Balls, East Indian, 68
    Croquettes, 68
    Ham and Mushroom Canapés, 45
    in Prunes, 74
    Mold, 90
    Snacks, 69
    Truffles, 69
    with Watermelon Pickle, 70
Cress and Caviar Sandwiches, 30
    and Shrimp Canapés, 39
    Butter, 22
    Stuffed Eggs, 83
Croquettes, Cheese with Bacon (cold), 68
    Finnan Haddie (cold), 60
Croutons, Fish Mousse, 32
    Gruyère, 53
Cucumber Cups with Salmon, 100
Cucumbers, Wilted, 83
Curried Crab Meat Bouchées, 111
Curried Lobster Canapés, 34
Curry Butter, 23
    French Dressing, 117
Czechoslovak Shells, 56

D

De Luxe Rings, 101
Dressing, Curry French, 117
Epicurean French, 117
French I, 116, II, 116
Mayonnaise, 118
Mustard, 119
Roquefort, 119
Russian, 118
Deviled Ham Canapés, 45
Shrimp, 63

E

Egg Sections, Stuffed, 72
Eggs Ravigote, 101
Stuffed, 83
Cress, 83
Horse-radish, 84
Lobster (cold), 84
(hot), 101
Olive, 84
Sardine, 85
Savory, 85
Smoked Salmon, 85
Eggs with Mustard Sauce, 86

F

Filling, Anchovy, 100
Cheese, 110
Finnan Haddie Canapés, 32
Croquettes (cold), 60
Fish Balls, 61
Surprise, Bacon, 61
Piccalilli, 61
Mousse Croutons, 32
Spread, 92
French Dressing I, 116, II, 116
Curry, 117
Epicurean, 117
Rolls, Stuffed, 79

G

Green Pepper Butter, 23
Savory Butter, 23
Gruyère Cheese Balls, 69
Croutons, 53

H

Ham and Chicken Canapés, 44
and Chicken Liver Canapés, 45
and Chicken Savory, 102
and Mushroom Crusts, 44
and Mustard Canapés, 45
and Ripe Olive Canapés, 45
Balls, 66
Bouchées, 112
Canapés, Deviled, 45
Cornets with Spinach, 76
Medallions, 46
Mousse in Aspic, 103
Mushroom and Cream Cheese Canapés, 46
Horse-radish Eggs, 84
Root, 10

I

Iced Vegetables, 77

J

Jelly, Tomato, 116
Antipasto in, 98
Crab Flakes and, 100
Rings, De Luxe, 101
with Sweetbreads, 106

K

Kumquats, Stuffed, 72

L

LIVER (CALVES') AND EGG
SPREAD, 90
and Mushroom Spread,
90
Bacon and Egg Turn-
overs, 112
Canapés, 46
Squares, 65
(Chicken) and Bacon
Spread, 91
and Mushroom Spread,
92
Canapés, 47
Canapés I, 47, II, 47,
III (Holiday), 47
Lobster Canapés I, 34, II, 34
Curried, 34
Pickled, 35
Medallions, 35
Paste, 92
Slices with Mustard
Sauce, 86
Stuffed Eggs, 84, 101
with Curry and Cress, 102
Lucerne Canapés, 53

M

MARGUERY CANAPÉS, 102
Mayonnaise Dressing, 118
Russian, 118
Meat and Mustard Spread, 93
Paste Canapés, 48
Rounds in Aspic, 103
Turnovers, 113
Mousse, Chicken or Ham in
Aspic, 103
Fish, Croutons, 32

Mushroom and Calves' Liver
Spread, 92
and Chicken Liver Spread,
92
and Ham Crusts, 44
Bouchées, 113
Caps, Stuffed, 72
Fingers, 56
Ham and Cream Cheese
Canapés, 46
Molds, 103
Paste, 93
Mustard Butter, 24
Dressing, 119

N

NUT AND CHEESE CANAPÉS, 51
Balls, 70

O

OLIVE AND CHEESE CANAPÉS I,
51, II, 52
and Sardine Canapés, 37
Stuffed Egg, 84
Olives, 11
Marinated, 77
Seasoned with Garlic, 78
with Cheese Shreds, 78
with Chicken Salad, 73
with Meat Shreds, 78
with *Pâté de Foie Gras,*
73
with Spiced Cheese, 73
Onions, Glazed, 73
Oysters and Spinach Baked
on Shell, 104
Baked on the Shell, 104
Farcie, 105
Fried, 61

P

Parmesan Cheese Sticks, 113
Parsley Butter, 24
  Crescents, 114
  Crusts, 114
Paste, Avocado, 90
  Chicken Salad, 92
  Lobster, 92
  Meat, Canapés, 48
  Mushroom, 93
Pastries, Cheese, 111
Pastry Stars (Caviar), 109
Pâté de Foie Gras, 11
  Acorns, 66
  Canapés I, 48, II, 48, III, 49
Peanut Butter and Bacon Canapés, 42
  and Celery Spread, 93
Pickled English Walnuts, 11
  Lobster Canapés, 35
Pimiento Anchovies, 80
  and Cheese Canapés, 52
  Butter, 24
  Canapés (Valentine), 58
  Stars, 57
Pimientos, 12
Prunes and Bacon, 64
  and Cream Cheese with Rum, 74
Pumpernickel Dominoes, 70

R

Radish and Scallion Spread, 93
  Canapé, 57
Radishes, Stuffed, I, 78, II, 79
Rarebit, Spanish, Spread, 95
Ravigote Eggs, 101

Red Butter, 25
Relish, Cabbage, 81
  Celery I, 82, II, 82
  Salad, 86
  Shrimp, 87
Rings, Antipasto, 98
  De Luxe, 101
Ripe Olive and Ham Canapés, 45
Rolls, Asparagus, 109
Rolls, French Stuffed, 79
Roquefort Dressing, 119
  Wafers, 54
Rose Apples, 12
Rusks, Savory Cheese, 54
Russell Canapés (Caviar), 29
Russian Canapés (Caviar), 30
  Mayonnaise, 118

S

Salad, Chicken, Canapés, 44
  Paste, 92
Salad Relish, 86
Salmon in Cucumber Cups, 100
  Smoked, 12
  and Cream Cheese Buds, 63
  and Cream Cheese Canapés, 40
  Balls, 63
  Canapés I, 39, II, 39
  Caviar and Anchovy Canapés, 40
  Custard Slices, 105
  Danish Canapés, 39
  Spread, 94
  Stuffed Eggs, 85
Spread, 94
Squares, 105

Sandwiches, Caviar and Cress, 30
Sardine and Olive Canapés, 37
    Canapés I, 36, II, 36, III, 36, IV, 36, V, 37, VI, 37
    Cuts, 62
    Ovals, 62
    Spread, I, 94, II, 94
    Stuffed Eggs, 85
    Whip, 94
Sardines, Broiled (Canapé), 38
Sauce, Vinaigrette, 119
Sausage and Chestnut Crusts, 106
Sausage, Grilled, 67
Savory Butter I, 25, II, 25
    Cheese Rusks, 54
    Ham and Chicken, 102
    Stuffed Egg, 85
Scallion and Radish Spread, 93
Scallops and Bacon, 62
Shells, Czechoslovak, 56
Shreds, Chicken, Indienne, 82
    Mexican, 83
    Vanderbilt, 87
Shrimp, 12, 62
    and Cauliflower, 71
    and Cress Canapés, 39
    Canapés, 38
    Indienne, 38
    Deviled, 63
    Relish, 87
    Spread I, 94, II, 95
Spanish Canapés, 54
    Rarebit Spread, 95
Spiced Beef Spread, 95
    Cheese, 91
Stuffed Beets I, 81, II, 81

    with Anchovy Filling, 99
Celery, 76
Cucumber Cups, 100
Eggs, 83
    Cress, 83
    Horse-radish, 84
    Lobster (cold), 84
    (hot), 101
    Olive, 84
    Sardine, 85
    Savory, 85
    Sections, 72
    Smoked Salmon, 85
French Roll Slices, 79
    Kumquats, 72
    Mushroom Caps, 72
    Olives I, 73, II, 73, III, 73
    Radishes I, 78, II, 79
    Roll Slices, French, 79
Sweetbread and Mushroom Bouchées, 115
    and Tomatoes, 87
    Canapés, 49
    in Tomato Jelly Rings, 106
    in Tomatoes, 107

T

Tomato and Bacon Canapés I, 42, II, 43
    and Caviar Canapés, 31
    and Sardine Canapés, 36
    and Sweetbread, 87
    Aspic, 115
    Canapés, 57
    Catsup Butter, 26
    Jelly, 116
    and Hot Crab Flakes 100

Antipasto in, 98
Rings, De Luxe, 101
Rings with Sweetbread, 106
Tomatoes, Sweetbreads in, 107
Trees, Celery, 76
Tuna Fish, 13
and Artichoke Canapés, 99
Turnovers, Chicken and Chutney, 111
Liver, Egg and Bacon, 112
Meat, 113

V

Valentine Canapés (pimiento), 58
Vanderbilt Shreds, 87
Vegetable Canapés, 58

Vegetables, Iced, 77
Vegex Butter, 26
Vinaigrette Sauce, 119
Volendam Canapés I, 55, II, 55

W

Wafers, Cheesehill, 53
Roquefort, 54
Walnuts, Pickled English, 11
Watermelon Pickle and Bacon, 65
and Cream Cheese Cubes, 70
Whip, Sardine, 94

Y

Yellow Butter, 26